Estrangement, Enterprise and Education

in Fifteenth-century England

THE FIFTEENTH CENTURY SERIES

Advisory editor: Ralph A. Griffiths, Professor of Medieval History, University of Wales, Swansea

THE FIFTEENTH CENTURY SERIES is a tribute to the vitality of scholarly study of the later Middle Ages (and especially of the fifteenth century) and to the commitment of Alan Sutton (now Sutton) Publishing to make its conclusions widely available. This partnership, which Charles Ross did so much to encourage, has been extraordinarily productive in the quarter-century since the pioneering colloquium on 'The Fifteenth Century, 1399–1509: Studies in Politics and Society' was held in Cardiff and presided over by S.B. Chrimes. The proceedings of that colloquium, edited by S.B. Chrimes, C.D. Ross and R.A. Griffiths, were published in 1972 (and reprinted in 1995). Since 1979 Alan Sutton Publishing has published a number of papers, invited especially from younger scholars and discussed at further colloquia, which have become a notable feature of the academic landscape in Britain. Aside from the encouragement given to talented young historians, noteworthy features of these volumes are the breadth of topics addressed, the novelty of approaches adopted, and the participation of scholars from North America and the European Continent. The volumes have proved influential and informative, and there is good reason to include further volumes in this major new series, both to recognize the achievements of the present generation of fifteenth-century historians and to consolidate the interest in later medieval history which they have undoubtedly generated.

This fifth volume in THE FIFTEENTH CENTURY SERIES is the outcome of a colloquium sponsored by the North American branch of the Richard III Society, held at the University of Illinois at Urbana-Champaign in 1995. The papers deal especially with the hazards and opportunities of public and private service in an age of civil war, and with the education and training of women.

ESTRANGEMENT, ENTERPRISE AND EDUCATION

IN FIFTEENTH-CENTURY ENGLAND

EDITED BY
SHARON D. MICHALOVE AND
A. COMPTON REEVES

SUTTON PUBLISHING

First published in 1998 by
Sutton Publishing Limited · Phoenix Mill
Thrupp · Stroud · Gloucestershire · GL5 2BU

British Library Cataloguing in Publication Data
A catalogue record for this book is available from the British Library

ISBN 0-7509-1384-3

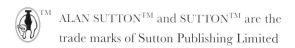
ALAN SUTTON™ and SUTTON™ are the
trade marks of Sutton Publishing Limited

Typeset in 10/15pt Baskerville.
Typesetting and origination by
Sutton Publishing Limited.
Printed in Great Britain by
Bookcraft, Midsomer Norton, Somerset.

CONTENTS

LIST OF CONTRIBUTORS

Ralph A. Griffiths is Professor of Medieval History at the University of Wales, Swansea. He has had many books published, including: *The Principality of Wales in the Later Middle Ages*, vol. 1, *South Wales, 1277–1536* (Cardiff, 1972); *The Reign of King Henry VI* (London and Los Angeles, 1981); with R.S. Thomas, *The Making of the Tudor Dynasty* (Gloucester, 1985); with John Cannon, *The Oxford Illustrated History of the British Monarchy* (Oxford, 1988); and *Sir Rhys ap Thomas and his Family: A Study in the Wars of the Roses and Early Tudor Politics* (Cardiff, 1993).

DeLloyd J. Guth is Associate Professor of Law at the University of Manitoba, Winnipeg. A pupil of the late G.R. Elton, he has specialized in the history of English law and government, notably in the late fifteenth and early sixteenth centuries. He compiled the bibliographical handbook, *Late Medieval England, 1377–1485* (Cambridge, 1976), and jointly edited *Tudor Rule and Revolution: Essays for G.R. Elton from his American Friends* (Cambridge, 1982).

Sharon D. Michalove has a Ph.D. from the University of Illinois at Urbana-Champaign, where she studied the history of European education with Paul Violas. She is presently the assistant to the chair in the Department of History at the University and an adjunct assistant professor in the Department of Educational Policy Studies, where she specializes in the history of medieval and early modern education in England.

Charles Moreton graduated from Trinity College, Dublin in 1986 and gained his doctorate at the University of Oxford in 1989. He has written *The Townshends and their World* as well as various articles about fifteenth- and sixteenth-century England. He is presently a research fellow at the History of Parliament Trust.

Philip Morgan is a senior lecturer in medieval history at the University of Keele. He has written on Domesday Book, gentle society and the Hundred Years War, and is currently completing a study of the early years of the reign of Henry IV.

A. Compton Reeves is Professor of History at Ohio University. He has recently written *Pleasures and Pastimes in Medieval England*, and his other works include *Newport Lordship 1317–1536*, *Lancastrian Englishmen*, *The Marcher Lords*, and *Purveyors and Purveyance for the Lancastrian and Yorkist Kings*. He is currently chairman of the American branch of the Richard III Society.

Colin Richmond has recently retired as Professor of Medieval History at the University of Keele. He has written widely on fifteenth-century England, particularly on the Paston family.

INTRODUCTION

In April 1995 the North American Branch of the Richard III Society held its first conference on fifteenth-century studies. The conference, 'Estrangement, Enterprise and Education: Chapters in 15th-Century English History', was meant as a 'prequel' to the annual International Medieval Congress at Kalamazoo, Michigan. It was our hope that this would be an international, state-of-the-art conference, and, although the number of attendees was small, our hopes were realized. We also hoped that this would be the beginning of a regular dialogue on fifteenth-century England in America that would parallel the fifteenth-century conferences held in Britain each September. The second of these conferences is scheduled for early May 1998.

The title of the conference incorporated the diverse selection of papers which were delivered, ranging from king-lists to political personalities to educational practices. The participants were from the United States, Canada and Britain. We hoped for, and achieved, a mix of senior and junior scholars. The papers in this volume are based on seven of the eight papers given at that conference. Professor Ralph Griffiths provided the keynote address. He put thinking on national identity in the fifteenth-century British Isles into perspective with his discussion of 'The Provinces and the Dominions in the Age of the Wars of the Roses' and his insights on the centre and the periphery led naturally on to the sessions that followed.

This was intended to be a working conference, and very few of the papers, as published, are exactly as they were presented. Most have been extensively revised. In keeping with the theme of a working conference, Professor Colin Richmond of the University of Keele did not bring a written paper. Instead, he developed some ideas on fifteenth-century politics that he had been thinking about and they generated a great deal of discussion. The paper presented here, 'Richard III, Richard Nixon and the Brutality of Fifteenth-century Politics', is based upon a tape recording of that discussion, with some judicious editing.

As the title of this volume indicates, the papers were quite diverse, ranging from politics to the development of a medieval civil service to the education of noblewomen. Philip Morgan's disquisition on fifteenth-century king-lists, '"Those Were the Days": A Yorkist Pedigree Roll', gives us some new thoughts on genealogy as well as possible insights into dinner-table conversation in the 1480s. Revisiting the Townshends, Charles Moreton discussed 'The "Diary" of a Late Fifteenth-Century Lawyer', giving a view of one of the relatively few personal documents to survive from the late fifteenth century, Sir Roger Townshend's journal, which includes lists of land purchases, a valor, and notes about a recently purchased manor as well as references to his activities as a justice, marriage negotiations, estate business and other events in the early 1490s. DeLloyd Guth considered the career of that very successful bureaucrat, Reynold Bray, in 'Climbing the Civil Service Pole during the Civil War'. He concluded that the essential character of late fifteenth-century England was not war but government and that Sir Geoffrey Elton's theory that the civil service began under Thomas Cromwell was dating that institution at least half a century too late. Compton Reeves told us everything we might wish to know about that successful prelate, Lawrence Booth, bishop of Durham and archbishop of York, in 'Lawrence Booth: Bishop of Durham (1457–76), Archbishop of York (1476–80)', while Sharon Michalove argued that upper-class medieval English women may not have gone to school but were certainly well-educated, in her paper, 'The Education of Aristocratic Women in Fifteenth-century England'.

We should like to thank the Departments of History at the University of Illinois at Urbana-Champaign and at Ohio University in Athens for their co-sponsorship of this conference, together with the North American Branch of the Richard III Society. In addition, Ms Kelly Gritten, currently at the University of Notre Dame, has been instrumental in assembling the papers for publication. Both the North American branch and the parent organization of the Richard III Society have been very generous in supporting the publication of this volume.

Sharon D. Michalove
University of Illinois at Urbana-Champaign

A. Compton Reeves
Ohio University

October 1997

1

THE PROVINCES AND THE DOMINIONS IN THE AGE OF THE WARS OF THE ROSES

Ralph A. Griffiths

I Harry be tho grace of God kyng of Inglond and of France,
lord of Ireland, prynce of Walys, lord of Gyan and Gasquyn,
Erle of Derby, Duke of Cornwayle, Erle of Chestre, Duke of
Lancastre and conqueror of Scotland . . .[1]

Whattttt gave the English state in the later Middle Ages its particular character? Some might say that it was the frequency and intensity of the wars in which England was engaged on the Continent and in the British Isles, for warfare loomed larger in England's experience then than at any time since the Viking Age. Others might say that it was the disputes among the royal blood about who should wear the crown, for such rivalries were more prolonged – and bloodier – than at any time since the Anglo-Saxon period. Yet others might say that it was the economic and social consequences of plague and demographic change, especially in the fourteenth century. A few might say, with justice, that it was the dominions which English kings acquired in this period, and the claims they made to yet further dominions, even to the kingdoms of Scotland and France. This latter view is, of course, intimately connected with the other three, but the relationship between England and the dominions, and its implications for the English state in particular, merit more attention than they

---

[1] Aberdeen University Library MS 123, f. 121. I am grateful to Deborah Young and Philip Morgan for bringing to my attention this capacious expression of the royal style, dated 1441, in a commonplace book written in the latter part of the fifteenth century.

have so far received. This relationship also bears on hardening concepts of English identity and also, though somewhat paradoxically, on an emerging conviction of an English superiority. This prompted, for example, Henry V's envoys to the Council of Constance to declare in April 1417 that the Scots, Welsh, Irish and others were part of the English nation too. The relationship also lies at the heart of the Wars of the Roses and the disablement of English government that occurred between 1450 and 1485.[2]

There is, seemingly, an incurable malady in English historiography which regards most developments of significance as having taken place within 30 miles or so of London and Westminster. Yet, although the Wars of the Roses were fought by rival royal lineages for the prize of kingship, few of the major battles or even of the minor skirmishes took place near the capital: Mortimer's Cross, Edward, earl of March's victory over the Lancastrians early in February 1461, occurred on the Welsh border; his follow-up success in March 1461 was won in bitter northern weather at Towton, between Leeds and York; and the Lancastrian forces were routed in 1464 in Northumberland, at Hedgeley Moor and Hexham. Edward IV's own collapse in 1469 was signalled by the battle of Edgecote, near Banbury in Northamptonshire, and were it not for his stalking of the Lancastrian invaders as far as Tewkesbury on the River Severn in May 1471, the victory he had just won over the rebel earl of Warwick at Barnet, admittedly a village not far from London, might have counted for little. The rebellion against the usurping Richard III in the autumn of 1483 was hatched by the duke of Buckingham from his castle at Brecon and came to grief in torrential rain in the Vale of Severn. And then Bosworth: we all know where that was fought, in the Leicestershire countryside 10 miles west of Leicester, even if some still quarrel about which bit of marsh and moor it took

---

[2] J.H. Mundy and K.M. Woody (eds), *The Council of Constance* (New York, 1961), pp. 340–1. On English identity and the Council of Constance, D. Hay, 'The use of the term "Great Britain" in the Middle Ages', *Proc. of the Soc. of Antiquaries of Scotland*, LXXXIX (1955–6), 61; A. Gwyn, 'Ireland and the English Nation at the Council of Constance', *Proc. of the Royal Irish Academy*, XLV, section C, no. 8 (1940), 183–233. A valuable context for this essay is provided by G.L. Harriss, 'Political Society and the Growth of Government in Later Medieval England', *Past and Present*, 138 (1993), 28–57, though it does not specifically mention the king's dominions.

place on.[3] Finally, the Irish invasions and risings against the first Tudor monarch, Henry VII, were crushed, first, in June 1487, at Stoke-by-Newark in Nottinghamshire, the invaders having landed on the Furness peninsula and made their way across the Pennines to Yorkshire; and later, in September 1497, when Perkin Warbeck and his south-western rebels melted away before the king near Exeter.

These were the critical engagements. Indeed, the few battles that did take place near London were not decisive ones: Edward IV's victory at Barnet, over Warwick and the restored Lancastrians in April 1471, and the two confrontations in the streets of St Albans (one of the penalties for being on the Great North Road) on 22 May 1455, when Henry VI was defeated and wounded in the neck, and on 17 February 1461, when Edward IV's allies were vanquished by Henry's queen and her army of northerners. The battles at St Albans were actually lost by the side that afterwards secured the crown. This was not because London, by far the largest centre of population in England, did not matter (rather, it mattered so much that its citizens and businessmen calculated their own interest and held aloof from fighting as far as possible); but because the armies of kings and of their opponents were mostly the retinues, officials and tenantry of nobles, roused by who knows what individual motives, including rustic and townsfolk's motives that were likely as not unconnected with the royal dynastic disputes.[4]

The early skirmishes in Yorkshire in 1453–5 between Percies and Nevilles, pulling in the dukes of Exeter and York, and culminating in the first battle of St Albans, were fought by local yeomen, tenants and village priests, as well as by manorial and estate officials and retained knights, esquires and gentlemen. They were all bound to one noble family or another by ties of mutual interest and duty, kinship, deference or tradition to serve their respective lords in their quarrels, even

---

[3] For a military history of the wars, with useful maps, A.E. Goodman, *The Wars of the Roses: Military Activity and English Society, 1452–97* (London, 1981). For the Bosworth dispute, and the most convincing account of the battle, P.J. Foss, *The Field of Redemore: The Battle of Bosworth, 1485* (Leeds, 1990).

[4] For the king's wound, J. Gairdner (ed.), *The Paston Letters*, III (London, 1904), 28. For London's attitude, C.M. Barron, 'London and the Crown, 1451–61', in J.R.L. Highfield and R.M. Jeffs (eds), *The Crown and Local Communities in England and France in the Fifteenth Century* (Gloucester, 1981), pp. 88–109, quoting Corporation of London Record Office, Journal 6, f. 251, in which the clerk of the commonalty noted (6 July 1460) that its primary concern was 'The security and defence of the city'.

when these quarrels were intertwined with disputes in other places and for different reasons. At the same time, Hereford's community was divided by competing interests that were dictated by personal, administrative and commercial rivalries, and as such they could be manipulated to advance the influence of Richard, duke of York in the city and to facilitate the realization of his political ambitions on a broader front. At the battle of Blore Heath, in north-west Staffordshire, close to the border with Cheshire and Shropshire, large numbers of Cheshire gentry and tenantry fought and died on 23 September 1459 in the service of their own Cheshire lords, be they Queen Margaret acting on behalf of her son, the prince, or the Stanleys or Lords Audley and Dudley: '. . . Blore Heath was a defeat for Cheshire . . . and demonstrated the strength of support in the palatinate for the Lancastrian cause'. In Wales the communities of shires and Marcher lordships may have been more cohesive in their loyalties to current lords, be they the crown in Cardiganshire and Merioneth (where Lancastrian devotion proved most tenacious), the Stafford dukes of Buckingham in the lordship of Brecon, or the duke of York in the lordship of Denbigh. Leading squires and landowners generally proved loyal to the lord under whom they prospered, and accordingly they were inclined to embrace his causes and ambitions when summoned to join him. Thus, at Mortimer's Cross in 1461, Jasper Tudor, earl of Pembroke led Welsh landowners and tenantry predominantly from Pembrokeshire and the royal shire of Carmarthen, whereas Edward, earl of March drew contingents from the earldom of March and the Neville lordship of Glamorgan.[5] In short, the Wars of the Roses were wars of the provinces and the dominions.

This suggests a serious failure of royal power and central governmental authority and control in the dominions and in those provinces towards the extremities of

---

[5] For the make-up of the Percy and Neville forces, Public Record Office, King's Bench, Ancient Indictments, analysed by R.A. Griffiths, 'Local Rivalries and National Politics: the Percies, the Nevilles and the Duke of Exeter, 1452–1454', *Speculum*, XLIII (1968), 589–632. For Hereford, A. Herbert, 'Herefordshire, 1413–61: Some Aspects of Society and Public Order', in R.A. Griffiths (ed.), *Patronage, the Crown and the Provinces in Later Medieval England* (Gloucester, 1981), ch. 5. For Mortimer's Cross, J.H. Harvey (ed.), *William Worcestre: Itineraries* (Oxford, 1969), pp. 203–5, with commentary by H.T. Evans, *Wales and the Wars of the Roses* (2nd edn, Stroud, 1995), pp. 74–80. For Blore Heath, D.J. Clayton, *The Administration of the County Palatine of Chester, 1442–85* (Chetham Soc., Manchester, 1990), pp. 74–90.

the realm. After all, the final victor in the dynastic wars was a quarter-Welshman and a quarter-Frenchman, Henry Tudor, who won his decisive battle in 1485 after landing from France virtually unopposed on the furthest tip of south Wales and recruiting Frenchmen, Scots and Welshmen on the way. Only at Shrewsbury was his way barred, some townsmen closing the gate and lowering the portcullis – for one day only! Henry's half-uncle, Henry VI, had been challenged at the outset of the wars by his first cousin, Richard, duke of York. As York's most recent biographer puts it, 'It was the earldom of March which changed Richard of York from a substantial landowner to a great one'; it could be added that it was these great possessions of his in the Marches of Wales, and also those inherited by him in Ireland, and the influence they gave him, that enabled him to strike at the crown.[6] To go further into the dominions, the hardest and most damaging nail hammered into the reputation of the Lancastrian monarchy was the final loss of Gascony in 1453; and when, initially, the Yorkist challengers were rebuffed by the king himself at Ludford Bridge, near Ludlow in Shropshire, in October 1459, they fled to regroup in safety in Ireland and Calais.

As long ago as 1926, that most English of English historians, G.M. Trevelyan, wrote:

> The Wars of the Roses were to a large extent a quarrel between Welsh Marcher lords, who were also great English nobles, closely related to the English throne.[7]

Few would endorse his order of priorities today, but he certainly makes a good point. And one might justifiably broaden the scope of his judgement. By the provinces one would mean the shires of England well beyond the capital, and

---

[6] For the significance of the earldom of March, valued in about 1424–6 at £3,700, and eleven of whose nineteen receiverships were in Wales and the Marches, P.A. Johnson, *Duke Richard of York, 1411–1460* (Oxford, 1988), pp. 7, 23–4. For York's Irish lands – the earldom of Ulster and the lordships of Connacht, Trim and Leix – and the popularity he won in Ireland, A. Cosgrove (ed.), *A New History of Ireland*, II (Oxford, 1987), 558ff.

[7] *History of England* (3rd edn, London, 1945), p. 259.

the palatinates of Durham, Chester and Lancaster. The dominions were Gascony, the Channel Islands, the principality of Wales and its Marches, Ireland, the Isle of Man, Calais, and, by claim if little else, the Scottish kingdom – all beyond the realm of England but 'parcels' (or separate elements) of the English crown.[8] All – and especially the dominions with which this discussion is mainly concerned – help to explain the phenomenon known as the Wars of the Roses, which disturbed a generation and challenged the stability of the English state.

The inhabitants of all these dominions were the king's subjects, even (it could be claimed) the Scots since Edward I's intervention in the Scottish succession crisis was invited in 1291. This placed heavy commitments on English kings that were encompassed by their overriding obligation to retain the dominions inseparable from the crown and to offer justice and protection to their various subjects. Kings who surrendered or lost a dominion would risk damaging the kingship itself, not to speak of their personal position as king; and this position would become even more vulnerable if other factors or opportunities arose to challenge it – as happened during the Wars of the Roses.

The problems and tensions arising from this obligation are clear. First, the distances were considerable. It took ten days to communicate or travel between Westminster and parts of eastern Ireland, let alone the countryside beyond, while the enlistment of forces, the commandeering of ships in Bristol and Liverpool, and the despatch of understandably reluctant royal lieutenants to Ireland could take up to two years – as the experience of Edmund, earl of March (1423–5) and Richard, duke of York (1447–9) demonstrates.[9] Ships bound for Gascony, which took months to prepare, often had a stormy passage in the Bay of Biscay and might just as likely make land in northern Spain or Brittany as at Bordeaux; it

---

[8] For 'parcel' in relation to Ireland, *Rotuli Parliamentorum* (6 vols, London, 1767–83), III, 231 (1388).

[9] The decision to appoint March as the king's lieutenant was taken on 2 March 1423, but he did not go to Ireland until the autumn of 1424: *Calendar of Patent Rolls, 1422–9*, pp. 123, 397; N.H. Nicolas (ed.), *Proc. and Ordinances of the Privy Council of England* (7 vols, London, 1834–7), III, 49, 67–9. York travelled to Ireland two years after his appointment on 30 July 1447: *Proc. Privy Council*, VI, 89; *CPR, 1446–52*, pp. 185, 227, 238.

took even longer to prepare a military fleet – if, after lengthy delays, it was felt worthwhile sending one at all.[10] It is true that news from Calais might reach London in less than two days, but (to take two other examples) news of the relief of Berwick from attack by the Scots took six days to reach London in July 1455; and Henry Tudor's landing in Milford Sound on 7 August 1485 was known to Richard III, 242 miles away at Bestwood Lodge in Nottinghamshire, more than four days later, the messenger having the benefit of the approaching full moon (14 August). Only in the reign of Edward IV does a regular posting and messenger service appear to have been organized, and then only to deal with the notification of exceptional events or news.[11]

The size of the dominions was another problem; together they far exceeded the size of England, and most were sparsely populated and not easily garrisoned. In Ireland there was a vigorous Gaelic resurgence that put large stretches out of bounds as 'the land of war' or under the control of 'Irish enemies' (the Gaelic Irish) and 'English rebels' (rebellious Anglo-Irish landowners). Bestride the old Anglo-Scottish border, English occupation in Roxburghshire and Teviotdale was resisted vigorously in the second half of the fourteenth century, and while English claims and ambitions did not diminish in the fifteenth century, it proved difficult to do much more than hold on to Berwick and Roxburgh. Even in Wales, in the aftermath of Owain Glyn Dŵr's rebellion in the first decade of the fifteenth century, peaceful behaviour could not be assured everywhere. Elsewhere, particularly if one stood in the northern borderland with Scotland, or in Calais or Gascony, or in the Channel Islands, there were hostile neighbouring states which were generally ready to exploit problems in the dominions or weaknesses

[10] M.G.A. Vale, *English Gascony, 1399–1453* (Oxford, 1970), pp. 137–53: the sorry tale of abandoned expeditions to Bordeaux in the crisis years, 1451–3.

[11] C.A.J. Armstrong, 'Some Examples of the Distribution and Speed of News in England at the Time of the Wars of the Roses', in R.W. Hunt, W.A. Pantin and R.W. Southern (eds), *Studies in Medieval History presented to F.M. Powicke* (Oxford, 1948), pp. 438–40, 445–6, 450–1 (reprinted in C.A.J. Armstrong, *England, France and Burgundy in the Fifteenth Century* [London, 1983], pp. 106–8, 113–14, 118–19). Cf. L.C. Attreed, 'A New Source for Perkin Warbeck's Invasion of 1497', *Medieval Studies*, XLVIII (1986), 515–16, for Henry VII's widespread use of posts for communication.

in the régime in England. The French, the Scots, and sometimes the Burgundians regarded the English and their kings as 'the principal disturbers of the peace in all Christendom' (as King James II of Scotland put it in 1456).[12]

The costs of the dominions in the fifteenth century were prodigious and the balance of financial and commercial advantage which had once been in England's favour was turning into a net loss. Irish horses or hobbies were still imported, the drover trade in cattle from north and mid-Wales to the English Midlands flourished, the wool staple and minting facilities at Calais continued, and the Gascon wine trade was reasonably healthy when not disrupted by campaigning armies careering through the vineyards. But income from the contracting areas of secure English control in Ireland, from aristocratic and royal properties in post-Glyn Dŵr Wales, even from the wool trade through Calais, was often exceeded by the costs of administration and defence, and it was proving difficult to reverse this trend. To take one example, in 1441 it was reported that 'the charges of the Justice of Irland [the head of the royal administration] and his officers this yere exceden the revenues of the same land, £1,456 18s. 1d.'[13] To take another, in Gascony income decisively exceeded expenditure in only one four-year period (1427–31) during the entire first half of the fifteenth century. And in the 1450s and 1460s there was very little margin of profit between the annual gross revenue of the king's principality of south Wales and its necessary expenditure.[14] In short, the dominions were expected to finance their own rule at a time when the tax regimen in England could not be expected to assist.

[12] J. Stevenson (ed.), *Letters and Papers Illustrative of the Wars of the English in France During the Reign of Henry the Sixth* (2 vols in 3, Rolls Series, 1861–4), I, 325. Cf. A. Goodman, 'The Anglo-Scottish Marches in the Fifteenth Century', in R.A. Mason (ed.), *Scotland and England, 1286–1815* (Edinburgh, 1987), pp. 21–2.

[13] *Proc. Privy Council*, V, 323. See, more generally, E. Matthew, 'The Financing of the Lordship of Ireland under Henry V and Henry VI', in A.J. Pollard (ed.), *Property and Politics: Essays in Later Medieval English History* (Gloucester, 1984), pp. 97–115.

[14] Vale, *English Gascony*, p. 235 (receipts and expenses of the constables of Bordeaux, the chief financial officer of Gascony). In all other periods, the accounts were in substantial deficit, with the exception of 1442–6, when income exceeded expenditure by a very small margin. See also R.A. Griffiths, 'Royal Government in the Southern Counties of the Principality of Wales, 1422–1485' (unpublished University of Bristol Ph.D. thesis, 1962), p. 496, based on a study of officials' accounts, 1422–85.

Finding itself increasingly on the defensive in its dominions, the crown nevertheless had to satisfy the expectations and ambitions of the leaders of the élites of local communities, whether they were Anglo-Irish knights and esquires, the native and immigrant gentry of Wales, or local mandarins in Jersey and Guernsey, all of whom vied for local prominence and gradually gathered into their hands the offices of local government and social control – as, of course, was common in the provinces of England too. These people might not be present or represented in the English parliament, but that was no hindrance to their growing power in their own localities and regions and may even have been an advantage in matters of law enforcement and personal accountability.

Another factor was the presence in Ireland, Wales, Gascony and, after 1406, in the Isle of Man of powerful, hereditary nobility, some of whom were resident from time to time and who always regarded their estates and interests in the dominions jealously. They enjoyed considerable incomes; rights of patronage in offices, properties and churches, to favour whomsoever they chose; and reservoirs of retainers, and castles of refuge.[15] These were sensitive people whose independence and autonomy wise kings would wish to respect. At least in Ireland and Gascony and in the northern Marches towards Scotland, there was the possibility of despatching royal representatives of standing and authority: royal lieutenants in Ireland, seneschals to Gascony, and wardens of both east and west Marches. In morcellated Wales there was nothing quite comparable: temporary interventions by Henry IV and (from 1406) his son, Prince Henry, were not repeated after the Glyn Dŵr emergency had passed, and in any case, between 1413 and 1509 there was a prince of Wales for only thirty-seven years and at no time was he an adult. The 'government deficit' in the relationship between Westminster and Wales was appreciated from time to time, and, faced with the dangers of continuing civil war in the 1460s and 1470s, Edward IV tried to deal with it. In earlier decades, however, identification of the problem did not produce

---

[15] In April 1406, the Isle (or 'kingdom') of Man was granted in perpetuity to Sir John Stanley and his heirs; Stanley's grandson was raised to the peerage early in 1456. G.E.C., *The Complete Peerage* (12 vols in 13, London, 1910–59), XII, i, 248–50.

imaginative, radical or practical solutions. The ineffectiveness of traditional and customary methods of supervision and control was evident by the 1430s and 1440s. On 21 November 1436 royal castle-constables and the two chamberlains (or financial officers) of the principality shires of Wales were instructed to go to their posts, and the Marcher lords to attend to their lordships and hold their courts regularly.[16]

At the same time, the problem of Wales as a whole seems to have occupied the attention of the king's Council at the outset of Henry VI's majority rule, and in a more fundamental fashion. There is some indication that a means of dealing with it in other than a piecemeal fashion was being contemplated. In November 1437 it was decided that the Marcher lords should be summoned to a general council meeting soon after February and 'that they be well with as touching the good governance of Wales'. The 'articles of Wales' which were delivered to the chancellor of England on 9 May 1438 may have been the outcome of such a meeting.[17] Little seems to have been done in practice, for continuing disorder prompted an instruction on 8 October 1442 to examine the statutes of Edward I, which had outlined the king's responsibilities and prerogatives in respect of all his subjects, in Wales and the Marches as elsewhere. At the same time, the Marcher lords were summoned to London to 'ordain by one assent remedy against the riots etc. in Wales before Christmas next'. The seriousness of the situation, as perceived by the king's government, is reflected in Henry VI's threat that if they did nothing then he would intervene himself in the lordships – a radical proposal indeed.[18] The next day, 9 October (such was the sense of urgency), the Marcher

---

[16] *Proc. Privy Council*, V, 5.

[17] *Ibid.*, V, 81–2, 92, 95. These 'articles' have not so far been located. On 22 January 1438 the king's remembrancer at the Exchequer was paid 20*s* for writing out the 'Statutes of Wales' for the king's use, perhaps to provide some of the principles for intended action: F. Devon (ed.), *Issues of the Exchequer, Henry III – Henry VI* (London, 1837), p. 434.

[18] *Proc. Privy Council*, V, 210–11, 213, 215. It may be relevant that only Humphrey, duke of Gloucester, and the earl of Stafford among the Marcher lords were king's councillors between 1437 and 1444, and Gloucester was rapidly losing influence. Cf. R.A. Griffiths, *The Reign of King Henry VI* (London, 1981), pp. 278–82.

lords were instructed to assemble in London on 18 November, well before Christmas, and to bring with them the 'notablest of their lordships', a revealing indication of the prominence enjoyed by the leading gentry of the Marches. Yet little of permanent value or of a radical nature seems to have been accomplished in practice. In 1442 the justices of the peace in the English border counties were authorized to try Welsh raiders provided an appeal to the relevant Marcher lords had been made and had failed – though these lords should nevertheless receive any forfeitures that might result and the statute was to last for only six years.[19] Henry VI's government balked at a frontal assault on Marcher custom and privilege.

An important question is this: how effective was the overarching supervisory power of the crown? To keep all these dominions under control, to keep the interests of local gentry, nobility and crown in an acceptable balance, and to keep external threats at bay, was not easy. The trouble was that by the middle of the fifteenth century the tensions and difficulties inherent in the king's obligations in the dominions were almost beyond the king's capacity to discharge. Henry V added one massive obligation to all the rest. By the treaty of Troyes with King Charles VI of France in 1420, whereby Henry and his successors would mount the French throne once Charles was dead, the warrior king not only extended the obligations of the English king to Normandy and its environs, which he had conquered, but also committed himself and his successors to winning the remainder of France. It was an impossible task in terms of finance and manpower, administration and defence, and the commitment ran counter to certain opinion in England and especially in France, where the rightful king was widely regarded as Charles VI's son, Charles. Reservations about the implications of the treaty of Troyes were expressed soon after it was concluded and known in England. A dozen or so years later, these reservations were shared by an influential group of councillors who advocated peace with France, a policy which Henry VI himself embraced.[20] The realm of France was a daunting legacy

[19] *Rot. Parl.*, IV, 53–4; *Statutes of the Realm*, II, 317–18.
[20] *Rot. Parl.*, IV, 127 (1420); C.T. Allmand, *Henry V* (London, 1992), pp. 146–50, 376–7.

to Henry VI of a sort that no other English king had been called on to shoulder, not even his father, who died seven weeks before Charles VI's death (21 October 1422), and who therefore was never king of France himself. Henry V, it could be said, by his military and diplomatic successes and his early death, threatened the entire edifice of the English dominions and thereby imperilled his own dynasty and the peace of England.

All these obligations and tensions lie at the heart of the Wars of the Roses, and they played a crucial role in enabling Richard, duke of York to challenge the crown by 1459–60. Equally, they confronted the new Yorkist régime with immense problems; while Henry Tudor's appreciation of these obligations and some of their dangers helped to set the tone of his reign after 1485.

Disillusion and discontent in the provinces and dominions were responsible for some of the more dangerous fissures in noble and urban society in England. Few would seriously doubt that the failure of Henry VI's efforts in the 1440s to conclude peace with the French, and thereby have a chance of preserving at least part of his Continental dominions – notably Calais, Normandy and Gascony – was at the heart of the Lancastrian dynasty's collapse in the 1450s. Henry and his government failed to protect the crown's French subjects, their commercial interests – especially the vital wine trade, mostly in claret, between Bordeaux and Bristol – and the commercial interests of English merchants and the estates of English families across the Channel. The weight of taxation to finance expeditions had grown heavier in recent decades and seemed all the more crushing when armies were defeated; and this taxation had fallen increasingly on English taxpayers rather than on the French dominions themselves. Then, when the inhabitants of south-eastern England witnessed soldiers limping forlorn and beaten through their streets and lanes, the resentment against Henry's government mounted and was expressed through popular and parliamentary protests by 1449–50.[21]

---

[21] These themes are fully explored in Griffiths, *Henry VI*, and B.P. Wolffe, *Henry VI* (London, 1981).

In Wales and Ireland, rival noble families had valuable lordships: the Yorkists in Ulster and the loyal Butler earls of Ormond and Wiltshire further south; the duke of York and the earl of Warwick in the Welsh Marches, but also the Lancastrian duke of Buckingham between them at Newport and Brecon, and the crown itself in the principality shires and Cheshire. With local loyalties to local lords paramount, the government did not have the resources or the personnel, or even the will, to assert its authority at such distances and over lordships and shires that enjoyed a marked degree of independence and practical autonomy. In the northern borderland, the financial and logistical problems were just as formidable, and were accentuated by similar noble divisions between, especially, the Nevilles, who came to support Richard, duke of York, and the Percy earls of Northumberland, who consequently clung to Lancaster. And at the same time the Scots could be relied on to take whatever advantage they could of problems and preoccupations south of the border, preferably to seize key fortresses like Roxburgh and Berwick. Shakespeare, taking his cue from the chronicles of Edward Hall and Raphael Holinshed, realized that this ultimately was a consequence of English efforts to make real the claims to dominion over Scotland in Edward I's reign. Here, one of his lords addresses Henry V in vivid language on the eve of the departure of the expeditionary force that triumphed at Agincourt (1415):

> But there's a saying, very old and true,
> 'If that you will France win,
> Then with Scotland first begin':
> For once the eagle England being in prey,
> To her unguarded nest the weasel Scot
> Comes sneaking, and so sucks her princely eggs,
> Playing the mouse in absence of the cat,
> To 'tame and havoc more than she can eat.[22]

---

[22] William Shakespeare, *King Henry V*, ed. A. Gurr (Cambridge, 1992), Act I, sc. ii, ll. 166–73.

Nor was Calais, 'one of the most pryncypall tresours of the realm' and one of its 'twin eyes', utterly reliable. The wool merchants of this staple port, on whom the financial and, therefore, military security of Calais depended, were sullen subjects of the last Lancastrian king, and more inclined to look to the Yorkist challengers to improve their lot and the security of their trade. With the earl of Warwick installed as captain of Calais and governor of the Channel Islands, and energetically establishing his fleet's dominance in the Channel, in each of which capacities he won wide popularity, these vital footholds in France – Calais especially – proved critical when, in 1460, the Yorkists marched against Henry VI and seized his person at the battle of Northampton.[23] The *coup d'état* was planned in the Yorkist strongholds in Ireland and by Warwick in Calais. If the military and political co-ordination among them left something to be desired, it was nevertheless the combined attacks across the English Channel by Warwick and Edward, earl of March, and across St George's Channel by York himself, recruiting in his Welsh lordships along the way, that created the circumstances in which King Henry was ultimately forced from his throne.[24] The Yorkist revolution of 1460–1 was a revolt of the dominions.

In the crisis years following Henry's deposition in 1461, the attitude which his queen, Margaret of Anjou, adopted towards several of the dominions suggests that she misjudged their importance to the crown and consequently sacrificed her husband's throne for anticipated short-term advantage. She implicitly abandoned English claims to superiority in Scotland in order to secure James III's aid: fleeing to Scotland in 1461 in order to invade northern England with a Scottish army, and at the same time agreeing, on 25 April, to hand over the strategic border fortress of Berwick, hardly demonstrate a full realization of her husband's obligations or a sensitivity to the interests of his northern English subjects. Forced out of Scotland

---

[23] *Statutes of the Realm*, III, 632–50; G. Warner (ed.), *The Libelle of Englyshe Polycye* (Oxford, 1926), p. 2. For Lancastrian Calais and Warwick's 'care for Calais', see G.L. Harriss, 'The Struggle for Calais: an Aspect of the Rivalry Between Lancaster and York', *English Hist. Rev.*, LXXV (1960), 30–53; Cf. C.F. Richmond, 'English Naval Power in the Fifteenth Century', *History*, LII (1967), 8–9.

[24] For speculations about the Yorkists' plans in 1460, Griffiths, *Henry VI*, pp. 854–7, with further comment in Johnson, *Duke Richard of York*, pp. 195–6, 201–6, 212–18.

by Edward IV's diplomacy in 1462, Margaret likewise appealed to Louis XI of France, once again hoping to return to England with a foreign army; in return, she promised to cede to Louis the town and fortresses of Calais whenever Henry VI should recover them. She had already promised the Channel Islands to her friend, Pierre de Brézé, Louis's seneschal of Normandy, to hold independently of the English crown, and a French army landed in Jersey in June 1461, much to the distaste of the islanders.[25] Were these actions really calculated to consolidate the Lancastrian monarchy's support in these key dominions, or indeed opinion more widely in England? Berwick, Calais and the Channel Islands were touchstones of Lancastrian bungling in a desperate effort to unseat the unstable Edward IV. One wonders whether Margaret acted for reasons other than short-term advantage, or if she fully appreciated the significance of these dominions to the English crown.

In one significant respect Edward IV's task after 1461 of restoring royal authority in 'the parcels' of the crown had been made easier: the loss of both Normandy and Gascony by Henry VI (1450–3) had reduced the crown's practical commitments to more manageable proportions, and focused resentment at their loss elsewhere than on the new dynasty. And Margaret's surrenders in 1461–2 nourished such resentment directed at the house of Lancaster. Nevertheless, Edward made much of assuming the prerogatives and obligations of a kingship every whit as capacious as that of Henry VI, including (when it suited him) the French inheritance. Moreover, in Normandy and Gascony popular opinion for a generation expected that the English would return; indeed, Edward explicitly proclaimed his rights in France as the justification for his invasion in 1475. Sumptuous robes made of gold cloth, lined with red satin, were prepared for a coronation at Rheims, which was his destination.[26]

[25] C.D. Ross, *Edward IV* (London, 1974), pp. 46, 50; C.L. Scofield, *The Life and Reign of Edward the Fourth* (2 vols, London, 1923), I, 161, 179, 251.

[26] Scofield, *The Life and Reign of Edward the Fourth*, I, 116; J.R. Lander, 'The Hundred Years' War and Edward IV's 1475 campaign in France', in A.J. Slavin (ed.), *Tudor Men and Institutions: Studies in English Law and Government* (Baton Rouge, La., 1972), pp. 70–100, reprinted in J.R. Lander, *Crown and Nobility, 1450–1509* (London, 1976), pp. 220–41.

About the same time Edward began to publicize his rightful role as superior lord in Scotland, and the extraordinary (and ill-judged) grant of an hereditary domain beside the Scottish border to his brother, Richard of Gloucester, in January 1483 may in part have been a public affirmation of Edward's Scottish sovereignty. Certainly one objective of Gloucester's invasion of Scotland the previous year had been the recapture of Berwick and disputed territory on the border, and the installation of a pretender, the duke of Albany, as king of Scotland, who would swear homage and fealty to King Edward. Yet Gloucester's hereditary Anglo-Scottish palatinate threatened to undermine Edward's own aims and achievements there and perhaps, in view of its enhancement of Gloucester's already extraordinary power in the north, the future of the house of York in England too.[27]

Edward had already moved to recover the Channel Islands, and in 1468 Sir Richard Harleston's fleet was enthusiastically welcomed by the islanders of Jersey, who were happy to send their French conquerors packing; on 23 September, Edward reserved to himself 'the superiority of the same [Jersey] in as large and like force as it hath been in any of the days of our noble progenitors . . .'.[28] As for Calais, Edward had demonstrated his commitment to its continuation in English hands – especially the hands of the merchants who had financed him since 1460 – by appointing his brother-in-law, Earl Rivers, and then, in July 1471, his friend and the chamberlain of his household, William, Lord Hastings, as its royal lieutenant until the end of the reign.[29] The Yorkist monarchy thus attempted to re-assemble the crown's dominions and win the confidence of their inhabitants, and to forward its claims in Scotland and France in order to enhance its credit at home.

[27] *Rot.Parl.*, VI, 204–5; T. Rymer, *Foedera, conventiones, literae . . .* (20 vols, The Hague, 1704–35), XII, 156–7. For comment, see C.D. Ross, *Edward IV*, ch. 12; *idem, Richard III* (London, 1981), pp. 45–7; R. Horrox, *Richard III: A Study of Service* (Cambridge, 1989), pp. 70–2.

[28] Scofield, *Edward the Fourth*, I, 478–80, quoting PRO, C81/821/2555.

[29] Scofield, *Edward the Fourth*, I, 521; *Complete Peerage*, VI, 372–3 (Hastings, whose appointment was renewed for a further ten years on 11 February 1479).

Edward's reliance on close relatives and personal friends was also the key to his attitude to Wales – and in the English provinces too. It was an approach to government with a long pedigree. In his first reign, his father's former retainer and Edward's close associate, William Herbert, who was made a baron, no less, in 1461, was the king's Welsh 'master-lock' (as one contemporary poet described him), with unprecedented authority in both the principality shires and many of the Marcher lordships; he was raised to the earldom of Pembroke in 1468. In Edward's second reign, it was effectively his brother-in-law, Anthony Woodville, Earl Rivers, who had oversight of affairs in Wales, through the vehicle of a council initially appointed in July 1471 for the child prince of Wales. Edward gradually (from 1473) conferred military and supervisory administrative and judicial powers on Rivers and this council, in the Marcher lordships and in the adjacent English counties, too. These powers became the council's consistent commission as a result of the king's personal intervention at Shrewsbury in 1476 and by concluding agreements with the Marcher lords, though – a conservative trait this – as earl of March, not as king. There was novelty in this, but there is, too, the air of a Marcher lord and his immediate coterie exploiting his aristocratic position, rather than of a king with new thinking in his mind.[30] There were dangers in such an approach. The Herbert hegemony in Wales offended that great Marcher lord of aristocratic blood, Warwick the Kingmaker, and this may have been a significant factor in driving a wedge between Warwick and the king and precipitating the battle of Edgecote in 1469. When Edward IV died, somewhat unexpectedly in April 1483, aged forty, the Woodville mightiness in Wales and the Marches seemed to accentuate political tensions with Richard of Gloucester, King Edward's equally powerful lieutenant in the north. Soon afterwards (in May), Richard III's elevation of his henchman, the Marcher baron,

---

[30] R.A. Griffiths, 'Wales and the Marches', in S.B. Chrimes, C.D. Ross and R.A. Griffiths (eds), *Fifteenth-Century England* (2nd edn, Stroud, 1995), pp. 158–62, quoting the poet, Lewys Glyn Cothi (D. Johnston [ed.], *Gwaith Lewys Glyn Cothi* [Cardiff, 1995], no. 112, and W.G. Lewis, 'Herbertiaid Rhaglan fel Noddwyr Beirdd yn y Bymthegfed Ganrif a Dechrau'r Unfed Ganrif ar Bymtheg', *Trans. Cymmrodorion Soc.*, 1986, pp. 33–60, for Herbert's popularity among Welsh poets).

Henry Stafford, duke of Buckingham, to succeed the Woodvilles as virtual viceroy in Wales proved a monumental blunder with dire consequences for Richard himself, for some months later Buckingham rebelled.[31]

Nor did matters turn out well in Ireland. There, Edward succeeded his father as earl of Ulster nine weeks before he became king. Richard, duke of York had earlier sought to consolidate his position in Ireland in 1459–60 by making concessions to the legislative claims of the Irish Parliament and to Irish administrative separatism. Edward, as king, found himself trapped by these concessions, and during his reign he could do little but act as a distant lord of Ireland whose practical authority stemmed from his lordship of Ulster and who perforce relied on the Anglo-Irish nobility. Edward's attempt to re-assert royal control by the appointment of his trusted servant, John Tiptoft, earl of Worcester, as chief governor of Ireland in 1467 backfired when, in 1468, Worcester sought to bludgeon the Irish into obedience by declaring the earls of Desmond and Kildare to be traitors and beheading Desmond ten days later. This was widely regarded as a major blunder and it helped to make Ireland and its nobility more, rather than less, intractable.[32] In their anxiety to re-assemble the so-called 'parcels' of the English crown, the Yorkists fortified the inclination towards independence in one of the greatest of them, Ireland, and embittered the Anglo-Irish nobility in the process.

When Henry Tudor battled with Richard III at Bosworth Field on 22 August 1485, he was, at the age of twenty-eight, more than half way through his life. Yet his first-hand knowledge of England – even of Wales and the Marches where he had spent almost all of his first fourteen years, from 1461 to 1470, in the Herbert household at Raglan Castle – was sketchy. He knew few people of any

---

[31] T.B. Pugh (ed.), *Glamorgan County History*, vol. III: *The Middle Ages* (Cardiff, 1971), pp. 196–9; D.A.L. Morgan, 'The King's Affinity in the Polity of Yorkist England', *Trans. Royal Hist. Soc.*, 5th series, XXVI (1973), 17–21. C.F. Richmond notes the problems created by Edward IV's 'land policy' in certain English provincial contexts: '1485 and all that, or what was going on at the Battle of Bosworth', in P.W. Hammond (ed.), *Richard III: Loyalty, Lordship and Law* (London, 1986), pp. 185–6.

[32] Cosgrove, *New History of Ireland*, II, 564–6, 593–612.

consequence in England or the dominions, except his fellow exiles in Brittany, who were few in number before the failure of Buckingham's rebellion in November 1483 caused others to flee and join him. These exiles were led by Henry's uncle, Jasper Tudor, earl of Pembroke, who was unusually well informed about the king's dominions, several of which he had visited as a Lancastrian 'terrorist' during the 1460s. Henry also corresponded with his mother's latest husband, Thomas, Lord Stanley, who was powerful in north-west England and north Wales, and was king of Man. And at Calais before 1485 Henry's allies had been intriguing with such effect that part of the colony deserted to Henry, and Richard became deeply mistrustful of its loyalty.[33] It seemed that the successful assault from the dominions in 1460 was about to be repeated. Alarmed, in June 1485 Richard III denounced Henry publicly as being ready, in order to achieve his conquest of England, to surrender to Charles VIII, 'callyng hymself Kyng of Fraunce' (and here Richard skilfully kept alive his own claim to be the rightful French king), not only the English claim to the French crown but also to Gascony and Calais and its Marches more specifically. Henry (he implied) would abandon an essential interest of the crown, namely, the dominions – just as Margaret of Anjou had been prepared to do twenty years before.[34]

What Henry Tudor did observe while he was in exile in Brittany and, then, briefly, at the French court was the threat posed to ducal and royal authority by powerful and ambitious noblemen. His consequent stern suspicion of nobility, combined with his appreciation of the importance of the dominions and the need, where practicable, to assert the full authority of an English monarch over

[33] M.K. Jones and M.G. Underwood, *The King's Mother: Lady Margaret Beaufort, Countess of Richmond and Derby* (Cambridge, 1992), pp. 42, 48; R.A. Griffiths, 'Henry Tudor: the Training of a King', *Huntington Library Quarterly*, 49 (1986), 197–218, reprinted in *idem*, *King and Country: England and Wales in the Fifteenth Century* (London, 1991), pp. 115–36; R.S. Thomas, 'The Political Career, Estates and "Connection" of Jasper Tudor, Earl of Pembroke and Duke of Bedford (d. 1491)' (unpublished University of Wales Ph.D. thesis, 1971), ch. V; Horrox, *Richard III*, pp. 279–80, 291–3.

[34] Gairdner, *Paston Letters*, VI, 81–4. For the importance which Henry Tudor assigned to the Channel Islands, derived from personal experience in 1484–5, see C.S.L. Davies, 'Richard III, Henry VII and the Island of Jersey', *The Ricardian*, IX, no. 119 (1992), 334–42.

them, led him to adopt a means of supervision that recalled Edward I's days: the despatch of king's servants – civil servants, if you will – under the king's direction, rather than the kind of aristocratic oversight that had undermined both Henry VI's and the Yorkists' rule. One of the shrewdest of contemporary observers, Sir John Fortescue, a lawyer and a former royal counsellor, rated highly a royal officialdom under the king's direct and exclusive control. The king (he wrote):

> shall haue than a greter myght, and a garde off his officers, when he liste to call thaym, than he hath nowe off his other ffeed men vndre the astate off lordes. Ffor the myght off the lande, aftir the myght off the grete lordes theroff, stondith most in the kynges officers.[35]

This coincided with Henry VII's thinking. Gradually at first, and then with more consistency than Edward IV had shown in the 1470s, he deployed in the provinces and the dominions his clerks, lawyers and servants of middling social rank, under his control (and his eagle eye) centrally. Indeed, he might well have preferred to place 'the kynges officers' before, not after, 'the myght off the grete lordes'. His approach may be observed in the palatinates of Lancaster and Chester, the principality and Marches of Wales, probably in the north country, and in Calais and Ireland too. Delegated administration, in the form of councillors – even by institutionalized councils – in Wales, Ireland, Chester and the north seems to have been combined with a conscious tendency by the 1490s to rely on experienced and dependable figures, laymen and a few ecclesiastics, rarely from the nobility but often from the relevant locality, who had a talent for effective administration, and who owed their standing and their prospects to Henry VII himself. These people strengthened the links between Westminster,

---

[35] J. Fortescue, *The Governance of England*, ed. C. Plummer (London, 1885), pp. 150–1. Cf. William Worcestre's lament in the 1450s that (in G.L. Harriss's words) 'The armigerous class was more habituated to office-holding and the courts of law than to the field of battle', Harriss, 'Political Society and the Growth of Government', *Past and Present*, 138 (1993), 53, based on J.G. Nichols (ed.), *The Boke of Noblesse* (London, 1860), pp. 77–8.

the king and his household, on the one hand, and on the other the organs of administration in the provinces and dominions. In Man in 1504, Henry at least required Thomas Stanley, the new earl of Derby, to surrender his title of king and revert to that of lord of Man.[36]

Henry was even more unusual in his attitude towards France and Scotland. He won at Bosworth with a part-French army and probably with about 1,000 Scots at his side, at a time when France and Scotland were still England's greatest enemies, and yet English kings advanced claims to be their sovereigns. Henry was in a cleft stick after 1485, as he tried to reconcile his personal inclinations and sense of debt to the French and Scots, with the obligations of a self-respecting fifteenth-century king of England. He managed, with some difficulty, to avoid outright war with France and he concluded, admittedly for security reasons, the longest-lasting alliance in almost two centuries with Scotland in 1502; this alliance was sealed in November 1503 by a marriage between Henry's daughter, Margaret, and the Scots king which eventually enabled James VI to succeed Elizabeth I and the claims to superior lordship to run into the sand.[37]

Elsewhere, however, Henry deployed the king's officers and servants to re-assert royal control. Yet, it has to be concluded that the Wars of the Roses hastened developments towards greater autonomy and self-rule in Ireland, Wales, the Channel Islands and the Isle of Man that were not completely reversed by the

---

[36] For some suggestions: J.A. Guy, *Tudor England* (Oxford, 1988), ch. 3 (esp. p. 57); Cosgrove, *New History of Ireland*, II, 613ff, 638ff; M. Condon 'Ruling Elites in the Reign of Henry VII', in C.D. Ross (ed.), *Patronage, Pedigree and Power in later Medieval England* (Gloucester, 1979), pp. 115–19; T.B. Pugh, 'Henry VII and the English Nobility', in G. Bernard (ed.), *The Tudor Nobility* (Manchester, 1992), pp. 87–8; T. Thornton, 'Local Equity Jurisdictions in the Territories of the English Crown: the Palatinate of Chester, 1450–1550', in D. Dunn (ed.), *Courts, Counties and the Capital in the Later Middle Ages* (Stroud, 1996), pp. 27–53; D. Luckett, 'Crown Office and Licensed Retinues in the Reign of Henry VII', in R.E. Archer and S. Walker (eds), *Rulers and Ruled in Late Medieval England* (London, 1995), pp. 223–38; B. Coward, *The Stanleys, Lords Stanley and Earls of Derby, 1385–1672* (Manchester, 1983).

[37] R.B. Wernham, *Before the Armada: The Growth of English Foreign Policy, 1485–1588* (London, 1966), pp. 27–61; N. Macdougall, *James IV* (Edinburgh, 1989), pp. 248–51.

centralist Tudors. For example, Henry VII's ordinances of 1494–5 to Jersey and Guernsey formally confirmed and defined certain powers of self-government that came to be exercised through the assemblies of Jersey and Guernsey; they guaranteed local liberties and custom, as well as affirmed the supervisory role of a distant king. This is precisely the basis for the present rule in the islands. In Wales, long-standing bonds of allegiance between communities and their lords were sometimes severely strained – sometimes broken – by the speed and frequency with which Welsh shires and lordships changed hands during the Wars of the Roses. This confirmed that resident élites would continue to rule the roost in their lords' place.[38] This was not an experience calculated to strengthen ties with those English nobles who were (largely absentee) Marcher lords, or with Westminster and the king's central government.

In the century and a half after Edward I's accession in 1272, the English monarchy had claimed and conquered very extensive territories and made them dominions of the crown at the same time as its government of England became the most sophisticated and effective in Europe. G.L. Harriss's judgement may usefully be extended beyond contemporary England to the crown's dominions: 'Government was moulded more by pressures from within political society than by the efforts of kings or officials to direct it from above. It was these pressures which shaped the institutions of government, the conventions of governing, and the capacity of kings to govern effectively.'[39] In both spheres there were tensions, pressures and problems of communication and control: in the case of the dominions, these tensions, pressures and problems were arguably central to the origins and nature of the Wars of the Roses. And as a result of those wars, important adjustments were made to relations between the crown, the dominions and the provinces. Had the English monarchy over-reached itself? Distances

---

[38] A.J. Eagleston, *The Channel Islands under Tudor Government, 1485–1642* (Cambridge, 1949), pp. 9–11; R.A. Griffiths, *Sir Rhys ap Thomas and his Family: A Study in the Wars of the Roses and Early Tudor Politics* (Cardiff, 1993), pp. 4–5.

[39] Harriss, 'Political Society and the Growth of Government', *Past and Present*, 138 (1993), 33.

were too great and royal visits scarcely feasible beyond the very occasional, brief tour outside southern England: Henry VI only once travelled as far north as Durham and never visited Wales, while no fifteenth-century monarch ventured to Ireland. Resources of finance and manpower were less than adequate in an age of economic difficulty, when the dominions ceased to make a profit and yet commitments were urgent and demanding on several fronts simultaneously. Separatist sentiment was strong, and even languages were perceived as administrative problems.

Historians have disagreed as to where to put the blame for the Wars of the Roses. Some have stressed the personal capacity of individual kings and, with fair unanimity, the personal incapacity of Henry VI; but could any king in the fifteenth century have coped successfully for more than a few years with both kingdom and dominions and, at the same time, advanced and realized claims to other kingdoms? Some historians prefer to stress the dynastic issue. It is true that the Mortimers had champions for their claim to the English throne from the 1390s to 1425, when Edmund Mortimer, earl of March died leaving neither son nor brother. Soon afterwards, by the 1440s, the Lancastrian monarchy sought dynastic security from Henry VI's extended family in default of children of the unmarried king himself; it was a strategy that came to coincide with the re-emergence of the rival Mortimer claim in the person of Earl Edmund's disenchanted and disgruntled nephew, Richard, duke of York, supported by equally disaffected allies. Yet dynastic legitimacy was consciously formulated and publicly embraced in high places at a comparatively late stage, more as a justification for the approaching conflict than as its root.[40]

[40] T.B. Pugh, *Henry V and the Southampton Plot of 1415* (Southampton, 1988), pp. 77–85; E. Powell, 'The Strange Death of Sir John Mortimer: Politics and the Law of Treason in Lancastrian England', in Archer and Walker (eds), *Rulers and Ruled*, pp. 83–98; R.A. Griffiths, 'The Sense of Dynasty in the Reign of Henry VI', in Ross, *Patronage, Pedigree and Power*, pp. 13–36, reprinted in Griffiths, *King and Country*, pp. 83–102. For the re-appearance of the name of Mortimer in association with rebellion against the house of Lancaster, see Griffiths, *Henry VI*, pp. 617–19 (Cade's rebellion, 1450).

Some historians lay responsibility squarely on the nobility and the greater gentry, their fluctuating fortunes and in some cases, echoing the opinions of contemporaries, their overweening power and ambition and their mutual jealousies. But if that explanation is to hold water, it must be given a territorial and governmental context, and the most satisfying one lies in the more distant provinces of the realm and the dominions. For instance, Richard, duke of York, and the Lancastrian duke of Somerset fell to quarrelling over Glamorgan in Wales and the supreme military command in France. The Percies and the Nevilles came to blows in the Vale of York for reasons that were largely northern, and, as we have seen, Warwick the Kingmaker's loyalty to Edward IV was strained to breaking point partly by his resentment at the Herbert dominance in Wales and the differences with the king over policy towards France.[41] Other historians note the delicacy of the relationship between the crown and the articulate subject – the political élites – in a monarchy that had become a co-operative and collaborative one. And, finally, others underline the importance of war – unsuccessful war or the lack of victorious war. This last certainly caused tension, but in his address to Parliament in 1472, the king's emissary, no doubt prompted by Edward IV with an eye on the brief spectacle that was Henry V's reign as well as the long discontentment that was Henry VI's, misled when he said 'that justice, peax and prosperite hath contenued any while in this lande in any Kings dayes but in suche as have made werre outward'.[42] Later medieval English kings directed their wars in too many directions in order to pursue, capture and preserve dominions: successful war could be as damaging to the monarchy in the long term as unsuccessful war in the short term.

[41] Cf., too, Richmond, in Hammond, *Richard III: Loyalty, Lordship and Law*, p. 183 ('English provincial politics may have contributed to what happened at Bosworth . . .').

[42] J.B. Sheppard (ed.) , *Literae Cantuariensis* (3 vols, Rolls Series, 1887–9), III, 282; cf., for the dating, Lander, *Crown and Nobility*, pp. 228–30. For a clear exposition of current views on the origins of the civil wars, see K. Dockray, 'The Origins of the Wars of the Roses', in A.J. Pollard (ed.), *The Wars of the Roses* (London, 1995), ch. 4.

Rather was the English monarchy over-ambitious and with a defective grip on changing realities.[43] It might have managed if it were growing richer, but it was not; or if it were more authoritarian, but it was not normally that either. Or it might have managed if it had cut its losses and drawn in its horns. Henry VII was inclined to attempt to achieve all three in some measure. Lancastrians and Yorkists, by contrast, tried – each of them, even Henry VI – to achieve one (rarely more) of these ends, and were prisoners of their own or their rivals' past.

This, in part, is what makes the age of the Wars of the Roses (to quote C.S.L. Davies) 'a crucial period in the history of state formation' – and, one might add, in the history of monarchy, which is what most states were in the fifteenth century.[44] It was also an age that deserves a place in discussions of the material foundations of state development. Fearful of the consequences for a state with a revenue inadequate for its commitments, Sir John Fortescue advocated a restoration and expansion of the royal domain. Had he, in support of his argument, raised his eyes beyond the northern Marches and Calais to other parts of the king's dominions, his advocacy might have been even more insistent.[45] One may say, too, that the history of this generation of civil war and crisis of crown authority suggests that chapters might fruitfully be added, albeit with altered bearings, to T.F. Tout's *Chapters in the Administrative History of Mediaeval England*.

---

[43] Taking a longer perspective, though confined to the British Isles, cf. R.R. Davies's conclusion: 'The structure of the precocious English state which had developed in the Middle Ages was, in the full sense of the word, quintessentially English; it has been part of its problem ever since to come to terms with the perception that Britain and Ireland are the lands of several peoples.' R.R. Davies, 'The Peoples of Britain and Ireland, 1100–1400: II. Names, Boundaries and Regnal Solidarities', *Trans. Royal Historical Soc.*, 6th series, V (1995), 20.

[44] 'The Wars of the Roses in European Context', in Pollard (ed.), *Wars of the Roses*, p. 184.

[45] Plummer, *Governance of England*, chs VI, X, XI. Cf. E. Isenmann, 'Medieval and Renaissance Theories of State Finance', pp. 41–3, and W.M. Ormrod, 'The West European Monarchies in the Later Middle Ages', pp. 149–52, in R. Bonney (ed.), *Economic Systems and State Finance* (Oxford, 1995).

2

THE 'DIARY' OF A LATE FIFTEENTH-CENTURY LAWYER[1]

Charles Moreton

Much written evidence about the fifteenth-century English gentry has survived, yet it is overwhelmingly impersonal, consisting largely of deeds, estate papers and the like. Wills are an obvious exception, but other documents of a more personal nature are comparatively rare and therefore deserve attention when they come to light. One such document is a journal found inside a notebook kept by a prominent lawyer, Sir Roger Townshend, in the early 1490s.[2] The bulk of the notebook is written in medieval Latin, although part of it is in a mixture of Latin and law French. (There is also a section in English, but this is not in Townshend's hand and may well have been written after his death.)[3] Most of the notebook contains nothing out of the ordinary,

---

[1] My thanks are due to my colleagues at the History of Parliament Trust for listening to a draft of this paper and making several useful suggestions.

[2] This paper is the result of a preliminary investigation of the journal, which I hope to edit in the near future. I am extremely grateful to the Marquess Townshend for allowing me access to this document, kept in drawer 58 of the library of Raynham Hall, and to the rest of his private archive over recent years. The notebook is some 11½ by 4½ in and consists of fifteen paper folios sewn into a parchment cover. The folios are made up of eight pieces of paper folded along their vertical axis. There are fifteen rather than sixteen folios because the original f. 15 has been ripped out, leaving f. 2 without a corresponding half. The cover has been folded over to hide its original text, some of which can be seen by peering between the fold. The name 'Thomas Howard, esq.' is visible, but it would be impossible to read the rest without detaching the cover from the rest of the notebook.

[3] F. 14 (part of a list of rents resolute on the Townshend estate which begins in Latin on f. 13v). The English continuation may well have been written for the benefit of Townshend's widow, Eleanor, since estate documents were normally written in English during her widowhood, when she was head of the family: C.E. Moreton, *The Townshends and their World: Gentry, Law, and Land in Norfolk, c. 1450–1551* (Oxford, 1992), p. 144.

although it provides invaluable information about the Townshend family in the late fifteenth century. Besides the journal, it consists of lists of Sir Roger's land purchases, a valor of his estate and, on f. 1, notes about a manor he had recently bought. The journal was written on ff. 2v–5r, of which 2v and 3r and parts of 3v–5r read much like a diary. Of particular importance is f. 2v, which contains notes he made about his activities as a justice on the home assize circuit during the Lammas (or summer) assizes of 1492. The rest of the journal is concerned with marriage negotiations, business on the Townshend estate and various incidental but interesting events.

Before discussing the journal, something must be said about its author and the assize system as it operated in his day.[4] Sir Roger Townshend was born in about 1435. Not unusually for a late medieval lawyer, he was of humble origin,[5] for his father, John Townshend, was a yeoman farmer from South Raynham, a small village in north-west Norfolk. Yet John was a prosperous man for one of his rank, since he owned two manors when he died in 1466. He was also ambitious enough to seek a legal training for his son, who was admitted to one of the London inns of court, Lincoln's Inn, in 1454. Roger was a good student and subsequently a successful and hard-headed lawyer. Using his legal earnings to buy land, he built up an estate worth over £200 per annum. The bulk of it was situated in Norfolk and was compactly centred upon the Raynham parishes, making it ideally suited for large-scale sheep farming, his main commercial activity as a landowner. In 1478 Townshend was appointed a serjeant-at-law, a preliminary step towards becoming a judge. Three years later he became a king's serjeant and he reached the peak of his profession in September 1485, when Henry VII made him a judge of the Common Pleas. Upon attaining judicial rank, he became a candidate for knighthood, an honour he received the following year. Townshend died on 9 November 1493, so his notebook dates from near the end of his life. He was succeeded by his son and namesake, the eldest of

---

[4] Unless otherwise indicated, all biographical details about Townshend are from Moreton, *Townshends*.

[5] E.W. Ives, *The Common Lawyers of Pre-Reformation England. Thomas Kebell: A Case Study* (Cambridge, 1983), pp. 30–1.

his six children by his wife Eleanor, the daughter of a Sussex gentleman, William Lunsford. The Townshends continued to flourish after Sir Roger's death, and joined the peerage in Charles II's reign. Perhaps the best known of his descendants is the second Viscount Townshend, who pursued his interest in agricultural improvement after he had retired from politics, thereby earning the nickname 'Turnip Townshend'. The present head of the family, the seventh Marquess Townshend, still lives at Raynham.

Upon becoming a serjeant-at-law in 1478, Townshend was liable for service as a justice of assize. The assize system was over 200 years old by this date, for professional justices had taken assizes in groups of counties, or circuits, since Edward I's reign. By Townshend's day there were six circuits: the home, midland, Norfolk, Oxford, northern and western. Two assize justices, drawn from the judges and serjeants of the central courts, would ride each circuit twice a year (except for the distant northern, which was visited only once) during the legal vacations which followed the Hilary and Trinity terms.[6] Within their circuits, the justices were empowered to hear and determine all felonies, treasons and misdemeanours and to deliver gaols. They were also authorized to hear civil actions, either through the archaic possessory assizes (for example, *novel disseisin* and *mort d'ancestor*) or by writ of *nisi prius* from one of the three common law courts at Westminster.[7] Townshend was assigned to his first assize circuit, the northern, made up of the counties of Cumberland, Lancashire, Northumberland, Westmorland and Yorkshire, in 1482. Six years later he transferred to the home circuit, upon which he remained until his death. His fellow justice throughout his time on the home circuit was Sir Thomas Bryan, chief justice of the court of Common Pleas.[8] The home circuit covered the south-eastern counties of Essex, Hertfordshire, Kent, Middlesex,[9] Surrey and Sussex. One of the most sought-after circuits in the late fifteenth century, it was also more convenient for

---

[6] J.S. Cockburn, *A History of the English Assizes, 1558–1714* (Cambridge, 1972), pp. 17, 19, 23; J.H. Baker, *An Introduction to English Legal History* (3rd edn, London, 1990), p. 25.

[7] Cockburn, p. 60.

[8] *CPR, 1476–85*, pp. 578–9; Ives, p. 68.

[9] Excluded from the home circuit in the sixteenth century: Cockburn, p. 53.

Townshend than the distant northern, for it was closer to London and his Norfolk estate.[10]

The first assize venue mentioned in Townshend's journal is Horsham in Sussex, where he sat on 23 July 1492. He recorded hearing two suits at *nisi prius* there. The first, involving two Sussex gentlemen, was brought by Thomas Combes of Pulborough against Simon Elrington, the son and heir of Sir John Elrington, a former treasurer of the household of the Yorkist kings.[11] It was a family quarrel, for Combes had married Simon's step-mother, Margaret, five years earlier.[12] Townshend did not record any details of the substance of the case, but the plea rolls of the courts of Common Pleas and King's Bench reveal that during 1492 Combes and Margaret were engaged as co-plaintiffs in at least two law suits. The first was against Simon Elrington and others for forcibly entering certain Sussex lands, and the second was against Simon's brother, John, for seizing £200 from Margaret. In another suit Combes, this time acting as the sole plaintiff, alleged that Simon and John Colt, Simon's brother-in-law, were withholding £300 which they owed him.[13] The second marriage of a wealthy widow like Margaret was not infrequently a cause of family quarrels. As Sir John Elrington's widow, Margaret was entitled to a life interest in part of his estate, meaning that her step-son, Simon, could not fully come into his own until after her death. From Simon's point of view, it must have been bad enough having one outsider, Margaret, in the family and even worse when she introduced another

---

[10] Between 1485 and 1502 the home circuit was totally monopolized by judges from the central courts at Westminster, of which Townshend was one when he joined it, to the exclusion of serjeants-in-law. By the early modern period, however, it had become the least popular circuit: Ives, pp. 67, 68–71; J.S. Cockburn, *Introduction to the Calendar of Assize Records, Home Circuit Indictments, Elizabeth I and James I* (London, 1985), p. 3.

[11] J.C. Wedgwood, *History of Parliament: Biographies of the Members of the Commons House, 1439–1509* (London, 1936), pp. 210, 297–9.

[12] *The Genealogist*, ns, xxiii (1907), 150, 153. Margaret was one of the daughters and coheiress of Sir Thomas Echingham. Her first husband, Sir William Blount, the son and heir of Lord Mountjoy, died fighting for Edward IV at Barnet in 1471: Wedgwood, pp. 86–7.

[13] P[ublic] R[ecord] O[ffice], KB27/923, rot. 8, 40d, 48; 924, rot. 15d; CP40/920, rot. 36d, 227d; 921, rot. 13, 23d; 922, rot. 8d, 14d, 153d, 182d. Sir John Elrington's will establishes Colt's connection with the Elrington family: PCC 8 Logge (PROB11/7).

into its affairs by marrying Combes. Fortunately for him, she died in November 1492, thereby ending Combes's involvement in Elrington family affairs.[14]

The second case which Townshend recorded hearing at Horsham was brought by Thomas Rookwood and his wife against William Lunsford and Thomasine Hopton. It must have been of particular interest to him, for the defendants were respectively his brother-in-law and mother-in-law. (See fig. 1, p. 44.) This may have been another family quarrel, since Lunsford was Thomasine's son by her first marriage[15] and Rookwood's wife was possibly one of her daughters.[16] Townshend recorded that the parties agreed to have their dispute referred to the arbitration of two prominent lawyers, Humphrey Coningsby and Thomas Oxenbridge, but, as with the Combes-Elrington case, he did not note what the suit was about.[17] Horsham was perhaps the most eventful venue on the circuit, for he also recorded that his white saddle horse (*caballus*) died in front of his chamber there, and that he bought a replacement, a bay gelding, from the vicar of the town for four nobles (26s 8d). Presumably the dead animal was not the only one he had brought with him: on at least one occasion in Elizabeth's reign new assize justices were advised to take six horses on their circuits.[18]

After Horsham, Townshend sat at Chelmsford, the county town of Essex. His entry about the assizes there is brief and refers only to a case heard at *nisi prius*, which the plaintiff won, without naming the parties involved. He did not date this entry, although he recorded staying the nights of 24 and 25 July at the house of Sir Thomas Montgomery, a prominent Essex knight who lived at Faulkbourne,

---

[14] *CFR*, vol. xxii, nos 108, 444. Even if Margaret had borne Combes children, he would not, after her death, have been entitled to a courtesy interest in any Elrington lands she might have held for life.

[15] C. Richmond, *John Hopton: A Fifteenth-Century Suffolk Gentleman* (Cambridge, 1981), pp. 101, 118n.

[16] Assuming that Rookwood had married his second wife, also named Thomasine, by this stage. (They had definitely married by July 1494.) There was certainly a strong connection between the two Thomasines, for Thomasine Hopton made Rookwood's wife a bequest in her will and acted as a feoffee for her and her husband. Possibly the younger was the goddaughter of the elder: *Collectanea Topographica et Genealogica*, ii, 135, 138; PRO, PCC Horne (PROB11/11); C142/35/29.

[17] To date, I have not found any trace of it on the plea rolls.

[18] Cockburn, *Assizes*, p. 53.

a few miles north-west of Chelmsford. As the distance between Horsham and Chelmsford is about 60 miles, it would seem likely that he left Horsham immediately after the assizes had closed there on 23 July, arrived at Faulkbourne late the next day and sat at the Essex town on 25 July. Yet by 26 July he had moved on to the Kent town of Sevenoaks, some 35 miles away from Chelmsford as the crow flies. There is nothing to suggest that he made a mistake with his dates when writing up his journal, so he must, as already speculated, have used several horses. It is worth noting that fourteenth-century assize justices also appear to have covered considerable distances in a short space of time.[19] Perhaps horses were sometimes kept ready in advance at points along the justices' route to ensure maximum speed. With regard to Sevenoaks, Townshend recorded that there was nothing to be done there, except to secure 'with much labour' (*cum multo labore*) an indictment relating to the murder of three boys at Dartford from the presenting jurors.[20]

Sevenoaks was the next venue after Chelmsford, but the chronology of Townshend's itinerary is interrupted by an entry which he made between his notes for these two towns. It relates to Guildford in Surrey, where a plaintiff traversed[21] an old assize, and is dated the first Saturday after the end of Trinity term, presumably 14 July, since in 1492 this was the first Saturday after the quindene of St John the Baptist, the date on which Trinity term normally ended.[22] As Townshend was still being issued with his assize commissions on 11 July, Guildford was probably his first venue.[23] He must, therefore, have written up his assize notes after the whole circuit had finished, rather than on a daily basis, but it is not known why he did not begin with Guildford. Townshend recorded that after sitting at Sevenoaks on 26 July, he stayed the night at Blore

---

[19] M.M. Taylor, 'Justices of Assize', in J.F. Willard et al., *The English Government at Work, 1327–1336*, iii (Cambridge, Ma., 1950), 236–7.

[20] Although Dartford itself was another Kent assize town, my earlier assumption (see Moreton, *Townshends*, p. 13) that the indictment was taken there rather than at Sevenoaks is wrong.

[21] That is, he formally denied a matter of fact alleged by the other side.

[22] C.R. Cheney (ed.), *Handbook of Dates for Students of English History* (London, 1978), p. 68.

[23] *CPR, 1485–94*, p. 398.

Park in Chiddingstone, the home of another former Lincoln's Inn man, Robert Rede, a serjeant-at-law.[24] It was about 6 miles away from Sevenoaks, which would appear to have been the last assize town on the circuit. The next day, a Friday, he was at 'Isle'[25] and on Saturday, 28 July, he arrived back in London. Beginning at Guildford and ending at Sevenoaks (assuming these *were* the first and last venues), he would have spent some two weeks on circuit. Over the next 100 years the assize circuits increasingly took longer to complete. By the 1580s the home circuit took seventeen days, from first to last venue, and the midland, which took thirteen to fifteen days in the early fifteenth century, as many as twenty-one.[26]

The Guildford entry is just one of several difficulties posed by Townshend's assize notes. Another is the problem of what he omitted, for there is much that he did not record about the circuit. He made no reference, for example, to his fellow justice, Sir Thomas Bryan, or to Thomas Gate, who was appointed to act as their associate.[27] What is more, he noted only a few of the cases he must have heard, and these, except for the Dartford murders, were all civil cases. Presumably this was because civil work was of greatest interest to him, since it was the most lucrative in terms of fees and was more intellectually stimulating than the criminal side of assize business.[28] Why he chose to make a note about some cases but not the many others he must have heard is another imponderable. As we have seen, these references are extremely cursory: it is only through the plea rolls, for example, that we have some indication of what the Combes–Elrington suit might have been about. It is also striking that he did not mention any venues in Hertfordshire and Middlesex, two of the counties on his circuit. Until the later seventeenth century, assize justices' itineraries often varied from year to year,

[24] E. Foss, *Biographical Dictionary of the Judges of England* (London, 1870), p. 549; *idem*, 'Legal Celebrities of Kent', *Archaeologia Cantiana*, 5 (1862–3), 28; Ives, pp. 474–5.

[25] I have not been able to identify this place, but Townshend does not refer to it as an assize venue.

[26] E. Powell, 'Jury Trial at Gaol Delivery in the Late Middle Ages: The Midland Circuit, 1400–1429', in J.S. Cockburn and T.A. Green (eds), *Twelve Good Men and True: The Criminal Trial Jury in England, 1200–1800* (Princeton, NJ, 1988), p. 82; Cockburn, *Assizes*, p. 25; *idem*, *Calendar*, p. 3.

[27] Ives, p. 68; *CPR, 1485–94*, p. 398. Gate was probably Thomas Gates, a lawyer from Bucks.: Wedgwood, p. 365.

[28] Cockburn, *Assizes*, p. 135; Powell, 'Jury Trial', p. 115.

particularly on the home circuit which contained a proliferation of possible venues and no obvious centres,[29] but such flexibility did not lead to the exclusion of whole counties. In any case, both Hertfordshire and Middlesex were included in the gaol delivery commission issued to Townshend and Bryan before the circuit began.[30] Assuming that Townshend *did* sit at Guildford on 14 July, he must have been in the missing counties at some stage between that date and 23 July, when he sat at Horsham.[31] All the same, this makes for a somewhat strange itinerary, for surely it would have made better sense to have travelled directly to Horsham from Guildford, a distance of only about 15 miles, rather than via Hertfordshire and Middlesex?[32] (See map on p. 38.)

Despite the problems they pose, Townshend's notes are interesting, not least because sources for the assize circuits in his day are far less abundant than for later periods (probably one of the reasons for the comparative neglect of the history of the medieval assizes).[33] They confirm that the circuits were ridden very rapidly: justices and their staff must have conducted business at each venue at breakneck speed and probably worked under immense pressure.[34] As well as considerable stamina, a sound constitution was a useful asset for an assize justice in this period, since there was a risk of contracting illness from sitting in cold or damp court rooms, sometimes in close proximity to disease-ridden prisoners.[35]

[29] Cockburn, *Assizes*, pp. 28–9.

[30] *CPR, 1485–94*, p. 389.

[31] Or did he leave those counties to Bryan, since assize justices did not always sit together? During the summer assizes of 1491, for example, Bryan was absent when Townshend sat at Horsham with their associate, Gate, but Townshend was absent when Bryan and Gate sat at Canterbury: PRO, CP40/915, rot. 131d; 918, rot. 329. But if Townshend did not sit in Herts. and Middlesex, what did he do in the meantime?

[32] A more detailed study of the plea rolls than I have yet had time to make may provide answers to some of these questions.

[33] E. Powell, 'The Administration of Criminal Justice in late Medieval England: Peace Sessions and Assizes', in R. Eales and D. Sullivan (eds), *The Political Context of Law* (London, 1987). Powell's 'Jury Trial' has some useful things to say about fifteenth-century assizes. For the early modern period, see Cockburn, *Assizes*.

[34] Cf. Powell, 'Jury Trial', pp. 82, 98.

[35] Cockburn, *Assizes*, p. 53.

Townshend's notes also confirm that fifteenth-century assize justices, like their early modern counterparts, lodged with the sheriffs and local notables in the counties through which they passed.[36] This meant that they were ideally placed to act as messengers between the central government and those who ruled the localities on its behalf, giving them an administrative and political, as well as a judicial, role. On their circuits they could communicate government policies to the rulers of the shires and, upon returning to London, carry messages from the localities to the king's ministers, for they reported to the council upon arriving in the capital. Their formal speech or 'charge' to grand juries was another way of making the government's views on various matters known in the countryside. Edward IV widely used such charges although, according to tradition, it was not until Elizabeth's reign that this practice was revived.[37] As assize justices visited their circuits twice a year and might remain assigned to them for a considerable time,[38] they were bound to become well acquainted with local politics and problems. This made them a useful source of information for the king, who would otherwise have had to rely solely on what the local rulers of the shires chose to tell him.

As previously mentioned, Townshend returned to London on 28 July. Although his circuit had finished, he continued his journal without a break. He recorded leaving the city on the same day and riding to Barking in Essex, the first of several stops as he gradually made his way home to Norfolk. He remained at Barking until the following Monday (30 July). While there he probably stayed at the town's Benedictine abbey, where his daughter, Agnes, was, if not already one of the nuns, soon to become one.[39] On Monday night he stayed with the

---

[36] *Ibid.*, pp. 9, 54.

[37] *Ibid.*, p. 9; J.R. Lander, *Government and Community: England, 1450–1509* (London, 1980), p. 37.

[38] For example, John Fisher served ten years on the northern circuit and then switched to the midland, upon which he remained until his death in 1510; Robert Rede served nine and a half years on the western before moving to the Norfolk, which he was still riding over eighteen years later: Ives, pp. 69–73, 462.

[39] She had definitely joined the sisters there by 1500: Raynham Hall library, drawer 58, memo. book kept by Roger Townshend II in the early 1500s, f. 10r.

sheriff of Essex, John Berdefeld.[40] Berdefeld's house was near Chelmsford and Townshend went into that town the next day. He did not record his business there or where he spent the Tuesday evening, but Sir Thomas Montgomery – with whom he had stayed while on circuit just over a week earlier – would appear to have put him up on the Wednesday night. The next day, 2 August, he arrived at the home of Edward Knyvet at Stanway, near Colchester, in time for dinner. The dinner was a family affair, for Knyvet was the nephew of Townshend's wife, Eleanor, and the other guests were Eleanor's brother-in-law, the Suffolk esquire, William Tendering, and his wife.[41] (See figs 1 and 2 on pp. 44–5.) While at Stanway, Townshend and Knyvet discussed plans for a marriage. Although the names of the couple concerned are not recorded, the match proposed was almost certainly a marriage between John Cressener, the grandson and heir of the Essex esquire, Alexander Cressener,[42] and one of Townshend's daughters. No doubt Knyvet was consulted because he was the young Cressener's stepfather, having married John's mother, Anne, after her first husband was killed at the battle of Bosworth.[43] Over the next two days, Townshend went first to Hadleigh in Suffolk to see William Pickenham, archdeacon of Suffolk,[44] and then rode on to meet Alexander Cressener himself. Presumably he sought Pickenham's advice about the marriage, for the cleric was yet another of his wife's relatives.[45] Cressener sought a marriage portion of 200 marks for the bride, but Townshend was prepared to pay only £100, in return for which he expected a jointure of lands

[40] Sheriff, 5 November 1491–25 November 1492. He held manors at Margaretting and elsewhere in Essex and died in 1497: *CIPM, Henry VII*, vol. ii, no. 1.

[41] Of Harkstead and Holbrook in south-east Suffolk, Tendering had previously been married to Thomasine Sidney (d. 1485), Eleanor's half-sister: Richmond, pp. 101, 129.

[42] Cressener's estates mainly lay in south-west Suffolk and north Essex: *CIPM, Henry VII*, vol. ii, nos 21, 84.

[43] R. Virgoe, 'The Earlier Knyvetts: the Rise of a Norfolk Gentry Family, Part 2', *Norfolk Archaeology*, 41 (1992), 271. John's father, another John, was Alexander Cressener's eldest son: *CIPM, Henry VII*, vol. ii, nos 81, 95.

[44] Archdeacon since 1472. 'One of the cleverest men of his generation', he obtained a doctorate in civil law in 1464, and had become rector of Hadleigh, Suffolk, by 1470. His Bourgchier/Yorkist connections possibly explain why he was denied a bishopric after 1485: Richmond, p. 216.

[45] *Ibid.*, pp. 153, 215.

worth £50 per annum to be settled upon the couple.[46] In other words, he was offering a portion which amounted to only twice the annual value of the jointure. Although the ratio of portion to jointure did not significantly increase to the benefit of bridegrooms' families until the early modern period (by the later 1600s, for example, it was normally 10:1),[47] Townshend's terms were steep, even by later medieval standards, and it is not known why he demanded them. It is quite conceivable (although impossible to prove) that he had some sort of financial hold over the Cresseners, for he had exploited the indebtedness of others in the past. Over two decades earlier, for example, he had won a manor from the Pastons after they had mortgaged it to him in return for a loan and then were unable to redeem it. He also secured several other manors on very favourable terms to himself by taking advantage of the unfavourable circumstances in which the vendors found themselves.[48]

The Townshend–Cressener negotiations highlight the extent to which medieval marriages were business transactions, in which several people besides the parents were involved. At the time John Cressener was only seven or eight years old (his proposed bride was probably about the same age), so the couple would not have had any real say in the matter.[49] In the event, no marriage occurred during Townshend's lifetime, although Elizabeth, one of his younger daughters, did later marry John.[50] The delay was no doubt partly due to the extreme youth of the couple. Perhaps the terms demanded by Townshend also proved an obstacle, although long and tortuous marriage negotiations were certainly not unknown.[51] Yet later medieval marriages were not always arranged,

[46] The Cressener estate was worth approximately £80 per annum in the 1520s: PRO, E179/150/251, 202, 248.

[47] L. Stone, *The Crisis of the Aristocracy, 1558–1641* (Oxford, 1965), pp. 646, 791; A. Macfarlane, *Marriage and Love in England: Modes of Reproduction, 1300–1840* (Oxford, 1986), p. 281.

[48] C.E. Moreton, 'A "best betrustyd frende"? A Late Medieval Lawyer and His Clients', *The Journal of Legal History*, 11 (1990), 183–90.

[49] *CIPM, Henry VII*, vol. ii, nos 21, 81, 95.

[50] Moreton, *Townshends*, p. 21. Townshend's will shows that Elizabeth was still unmarried at his death: PRO, PCC 2 Vox (PROB11/10).

[51] R.A. Houlbrooke, *The English Family, 1450–1700* (London, 1984), p. 84.

Places where Townshend is known to have sat are underlined.

nor did the couple concerned always obey the wishes of their parents. A famous example is that of Margery Paston who, by 1469, had fallen in love with her family's bailiff, Richard Calle. Although her mother and brothers were absolutely against such a match, Margery eventually summoned up the courage to make an open avowal for Calle and the marriage took place.[52]

Townshend's notes about his assize circuit and the marriage negotiations make up all of f. 2v of his notebook, except for a final sentence which helps to add to the diary-like quality of the journal. In it he noted that the vicar of Cley (a parish on the north Norfolk coast) was killed by lightning on 4 August 1492. There is no obvious practical reason for his interest, for he had neither lands nor advowson rights at Cley, so his fascination with an unusual death – the hand of God, perhaps? – must explain why he recorded the unfortunate cleric's fate.[53]

On f. 3r Townshend recorded his activities during the fortnight of 6–20 August. After his meeting with Cressener, he went to stay for five days with his mother-in-law, Thomasine Hopton, at Cockfield Hall, one of her manors at Yoxford in north-east Suffolk. A formidable matriarch, she had outlived three husbands, the last of whom, John Hopton, had died fourteen years previously.[54] While at Yoxford, Townshend discussed the proposed marriage alliance with the Cresseners and he took the opportunity to attend to various matters connected with lands that he held in Suffolk. He finally arrived back home at Raynham on Sunday, 12 August. Four days later he rode to Massingham, a nearby parish where James Goldwell, bishop of Norwich, had a house. He and Goldwell talked about a manor at West Tofts, of which the bishop was the feudal lord and which

---

[52] *Paston Letters and Papers of the Fifteenth Century*, ed. N. Davis, 2 vols (Oxford, 1971–6), i, nos 203, 245, 332; ii, no. 81.

[53] But was it in fact such an unusual death in those days? A century ago there were between thirty and forty deaths a year from lightning in Britain, as opposed to about three or four nowadays. Apart from the fact that we are now able to resuscitate many victims of a lightning strike, a major reason for the reduction in fatalities is that many more people lived in rural areas in the past and were therefore more likely to be caught out in the open during a storm: Greg Neale, 'Nature Watch', *The Sunday Telegraph*, 30 July 1995.

[54] Richmond, pp. 100, 118–19.

Townshend had bought two years earlier.[55] They also discussed the advowson of the Suffolk parish of Cleydon because Townshend was anxious to have it confirmed that the presentation belonged to his daughter-in-law, Amy (the wife of his son and heir, Roger), so as to thwart the claims of her step-grandmother, Elizabeth Brewes.[56] The day after meeting the bishop he had several guests, for Alexander Cressener, along with Knyvet and his wife, arrived at Raynham. They stayed for three days, much of which they must have spent discussing the proposed Townshend–Cressener marriage alliance. As soon as Cressener and the Knyvets had departed, Townshend rode to Castle Acre, where he was due to arbitrate in a dispute between the priory of West Acre and a gentleman named Coket. He recorded, however, that the arbitration attempt was aborted because Coket claimed that he would not be a neutral arbiter.[57]

After f. 3r Townshend's journal consists largely of estate memoranda, although a chronological sequence is maintained. Among other details, he recorded buying lands near Raynham from Thomas Thursby, a merchant from Bishop's (now King's) Lynn before Michaelmas 1492, on which feast day he was back in London, in time for the new law term. While in London he was involved in negotiations with other lawyers about a couple of manors. One of these, situated at Hilcroome in Worcestershire, was a property that he would appear to have possessed temporarily in the early 1480s.[58] The other, a manor in South Creake in Norfolk, was definitely his property, but the daughters and co-heiresses of William Beaufoy, the Rutland esquire who had sold it to him nearly

---

[55] *CIPM, Henry VII*, vol. i, 1143. Some notes about this manor, situated in south-west Norfolk, are to be found on f. 1 of Townshend's notebook.

[56] Amy was one of the daughters and coheiresses of William Brewes (d. 1490), the eldest son of Sir Thomas Brewes (d. 1482) of Fressingfield, Suffolk. Elizabeth, Sir Thomas's second wife, was the daughter of Gilbert Debenham of Wenham, Suffolk.

[57] Coket may have been John Coket of Ampton, a gentleman with lands in both Norfolk and Suffolk. If so, it is not surprising that he mistrusted Townshend, for his family had for some years claimed a right to a manor in Helhoughton, a parish neighbouring the Raynhams, which Townshend had bought, and did not give up this claim until 1495: *CIPM, Henry VII*, vol. i, 1007–8; Moreton, *Townshends*, pp. 85–91.

[58] *Victoria County History of Worcestershire*, iii, 320.

twenty years earlier,[59] were claiming that he had never fully paid for it. Unfortunately these negotiations are all that he recorded about his time in London during the Michaelmas term, for he did not make any notes about his duties as a judge of the Common Pleas there. Perhaps this was because his estate was his primary concern in late 1492: the journal shows that both before and after term time (he was back in Norfolk by 7 December) he spent much of his time scrutinizing accounts, court rolls and other documents, drawing up valors and giving orders for enclosures to be constructed, ditches to be dug and repairs to be carried out. He also reached agreements with neighbouring landowners, took stock of several law suits to which he was a party, and arranged for lands which he had recently purchased to be conveyed to feoffees. Medieval landowners often took an active interest in estate management, and Townshend was no exception. On one occasion a few years earlier he had scribbled, at the end of a sheep account, some scathing remarks about the performance of his ploughmen. He would appear, nevertheless, to have been almost frenetically active in late 1492.[60]

Townshend's journal ends a quarter of the way down f. 5r of his notebook. The last five lines are worth mentioning. First, he noted that the quarter sessions due to take place on Friday, 14 December at Walsingham, the famous pilgrimage centre in north-west Norfolk, were cancelled because none of the justices of the peace had turned up. No reason is given for their non-appearance, but perhaps he recorded it because it was an unusual occurrence. He then ended with the events of the following Thursday, 20 December, when he paid a rent he owed to Creake Abbey, a house of Austin canons situated near Raynham, arranged for his servants to receive their wages, and had an accident. He says he fell (perhaps from his horse, although he does not specify) and hurt his foot (in his own words 'hurt myne fote', the only English phrase in the journal) and, as a result, was unable to go to church between the accident and Christmas Day. Although he probably considered this a hardship (he was a pious man, if in a conventional

[59] Moreton, *Townshends*, pp. 119, 212.

[60] *Ibid.*, pp. 142–4. See R.H. Britnell, 'The Pastons and their Norfolk', *Agricultural History Review*, 36 (1988), 132–44, for the active involvement of the Pastons in the affairs of their estates.

sense),[61] he may have had the services of a household chaplain while he was incapacitated. Old age and infirmity were probably beginning to take their toll on him by this stage of his life, for he was to die within a year after this mishap. Perhaps the prominence of estate business in the latter part of his journal reflects his desire to leave his property in a good condition for his heir, who was still several years short of his majority.

In conclusion, what are we to make of the journal? Townshend may have found his notes about the prospective marriage alliance with the Cresseners and affairs on his estate useful, but what, if any, was the practical purpose of his entries about the assize circuit? They contain incidental details, like the death of his horse at Horsham, but, except for the Dartford murders, nothing of the substance of the cases with which he had to deal. They are neither a record of his fees and allowances from the circuit nor, properly speaking, legal notes. When he wished to, Townshend, who was a law reporter as well as a judge,[62] was perfectly capable of making detailed legal notes for his personal use and some from the 1480s have survived. Technical and written in law French, these bear no resemblance to his cursory references to a few of the cases he dealt with on his assize circuit.[63] As for the vicar of Cley, it was perhaps, as already suggested, the nature of his fate that prompted Townshend to record it for posterity. Of all people, lawyers were well imbued with the importance of records and record-keeping but, by the same token, were they not also among the best equipped to apply their skills to purposes which were not strictly practical? Whether many of them did so is open to question, given that Townshend's journal is certainly an

---

[61] Moreton, *Townshends*, p. 18. But one should not doubt the piety of fifteenth-century gentlemen: P.W. Fleming, 'Charity, Faith and the Gentry of Kent', in A.J. Pollard (ed.), *Property and Politics. Essays in Later Medieval English History* (Gloucester, 1984), pp. 41–2. For the example of Sir John Heveningham, like Townshend an East Anglian, see *Paston Letters*, i, no. 26; Richmond, pp. 235–6.

[62] A.W.B. Simpson, 'The Source and Function of the Later Year Books', *Law Quarterly Review*, 87 (1971), 11.

[63] Two papers in Raynham Hall library, drawer 11, bundle labelled 'HELHOUGHTON. Temp. HEN VI (1441–1460)'.

unusual find.[64] Nothing like it survives among his heir's papers: the second Roger Townshend also kept notebooks (three from the late 1490s and early 1500s still exist), but they are merely lists of memoranda.[65] Finally, is the journal, despite its diary-like aspects, really a 'diary'? Perhaps not; but in Townshend we surely see a nascent diarist.

[64] That is, as far as members of the gentry are concerned, although other medieval journals do survive: for example, that kept by Thomas Bekynton, bishop of Bath and Wells, while leading an English embassy to France in 1442: *Official Correspondence of Thomas Bekynton* (Rolls Series, 1872), ii, 177–248.

[65] British Library, Add. 41,139; Raynham Hall library, drawers 33 and 58. If the younger Roger ever kept a journal like his father's, it has not survived. One of his servants, perhaps acting on his instructions, recorded daily business on the Townshend estate between 1516 and 1518, but the resulting day-book is not a personal record: *'Skayman's Book'*, ed. C.E. Moreton and P. Rutledge (Norfolk Record Society, forthcoming).

FIG. 1: THE TOWNSHENDS AND THEIR CONNECTIONS

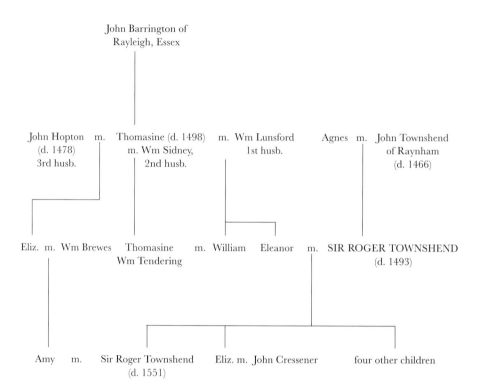

FIG. 2: THE TOWNSHENDS, KNYVETS AND CRESSENERS

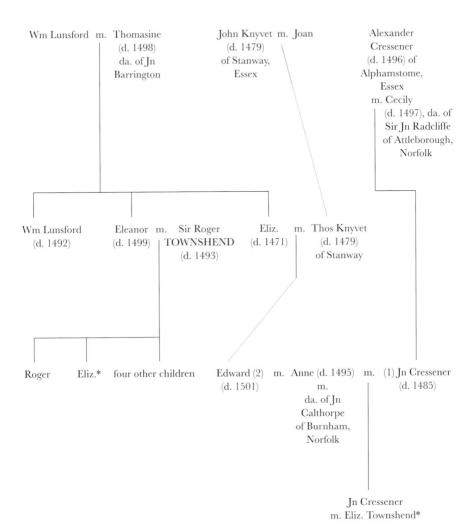

Wm Lunsford m. Thomasine
                 (d. 1498)
                 da. of Jn
                 Barrington

John Knyvet m. Joan
    (d. 1479)
   of Stanway,
     Essex

Alexander
Cressener
(d. 1496) of
Alphamstome,
Essex
m. Cecily
    (d. 1497), da. of
    Sir Jn Radcliffe
    of Attleborough,
    Norfolk

Wm Lunsford
(d. 1492)

Eleanor m. Sir Roger
(d. 1499) | TOWNSHEND
          (d. 1493)

Eliz. m. Thos Knyvet
(d. 1471)   (d. 1479)
        of Stanway

Roger   Eliz.*   four other children

Edward (2) m. Anne (d. 1495) m. (1) Jn Cressener
(d. 1501)   m.   (d. 1485)
        da. of Jn
       Calthorpe
     of Burnham,
      Norfolk

Jn Cressener
m. Eliz. Townshend*

*   Elizabeth Townshend, daughter of Sir Roger Townshend (d. 1493).

3

Climbing the Civil-Service Pole During Civil War: Sir Reynold Bray (*c.* 1440–1503)

DeLloyd J. Guth[1]

Did a civil service exist in late medieval England, as a mentality and as a reality, in a culture that can be accurately symbolized by a pole of competitive self-improvement? Did it matter then, and does it matter now? If an identifiable civil service did exist, it did so because of its *functions*. To define these, we must examine the late medieval vocabulary for articulations of a civil-service mentality: did people think in such terms? And we must peruse late medieval institutional records to document its reality: did people perform civil-service tasks? Here any public versus private, royal versus lay-ecclesiastical, jurisdictional lines are blurred; and most instruments for law and order were empowered by virtue of proprietary rights and obligations, firmly in the hands of servants of local civil authorities.

Pre-Reformation England was a rigorously governed place. The ordinary person had least contact with crown servants and most with parochial, manorial and municipal officials. Most encounters were with the governing landlady or landlord, and more likely their deputies, in roles of revenue-raiser, revenue-spender and summary magistrate. The impacts of such governmental functions on any individual would be muffled in the vocabulary of 'civil', referring to public and community order, and of 'service', meaning attendant duties and deferential labour. The royal centre of accounts and law courts at Westminster

[1] Faculty of Law, University of Manitoba. For their editorial patience, I am grateful to Dr Sharon D. Michalove, Professor A. Compton Reeves, Ms Kelly Gritten, and in this essay's final stage, Professor Ralph A. Griffiths. This work owes much to my co-editor of the Bray letters, Margaret M. Condon, who continues to apply careful scholarship to our project.

offered the apex for those most likely trained in the Inns of Chancery and apprenticed in the country. We need only pause to visualize the swarms of clerks, copyists, messengers, deputized collectors, writ writers, document drafters, tally notchers, filers and secretaries drawn to the many royal hives of central government. Literally hundreds had to exist at any given time to produce the piles of parchment, only a small portion of which have survived for us to study.

If much governed, in part because the extant primary evidence reveals a civil-service mentality and reality, then the theme of continuity becomes one defining characteristic for a society that is over 500 years removed from us. The existence of a civil service anywhere bespeaks that continuity, predictability and formalism that civil societies require. But, when we look at most of our modern historiography for late medieval England, it is built largely on scenarios of war, against the fleur-de-lis and between red and white roses, of dynastic crises both royal and regional, of a disease-controlled demography, of a corrupting clientage society and of an eschatological popular culture. The image of a war-ridden culture especially suits modern minds, numbed as they are by the universality of a twentieth-century warfare that has been totalitarian and indiscriminately civilian. Thus, to build our narratives around war and endemic social discontinuities has automatically created a presentist's grotesquerie of the fifteenth century.

The late Sir Geoffrey Elton, my doctoral supervisor, essentially accepted such scenarios and might have furrowed his brow at counter suggestions of themes of continuity, particularly any that posited a civil service extant before Thomas Cromwell and the 1530s. While he later modified some arguments made in *The Tudor Revolution in Government* (1953), he relied on a fifteenth century that projected dynastic violence, royal and local, and emphasized chamber-based administration, supinely dependent parliaments and service based on personal, not professional, credentials and connections.[2] Even as the twentieth century

---

[2] G.R. Elton, *The Tudor Revolution in Government: Administrative Changes in the Reign of Henry VIII* (Cambridge, 1953); 'Henry VII: Rapacity and Remorse', *Historical Journal*, I (1958), 21–39; 'Henry VII: a Restatement', *Historical Journal*, IV (1961), 1–29; 'The Tudor Revolutions: a Reply', *Past and Present*, XXIX (1964), 26–49; 'A Revolution in Tudor History?' *Past and Present*, XXXII (1965), 103–9; and W.C. Richardson, *Tudor Chamber Administration, 1485–1547* (Baton Rouge, 1952).

ends, that picture remains as a backdrop against which the Tudor drama is played, rescuing England from the reality of Lancastrian and Yorkist chaos.

For some reason, more recent scholars have avoided the careful reconstructions of what fifteenth-century institutions, royal and local, did and, therefore, also did not do.[3] If we knew more about that, then we might know who performed the necessary tasks: perhaps civil servants? Instead, professional historians and antiquarians have continued to produce many dynastic, regional, biographical, local, literary, textual and ecclesiastical studies. Most are in essay format, each as a conspectus, but few if any offer detailed administrative histories, certainly not since the 1960s made 'social history' the talismanic label for conjuring academic reputations. By stark contrast, in the first half of the twentieth century analyses of late medieval institutions totally dominated research and publication. The works of Tout, Dunham, Denholm-Young, Chrimes, Otway-Ruthven, Somerville, Steel, Wilkinson, Hastings, Blatcher and Wolffe,[4] among others, focused primarily on structures and procedures, mainly operated by civil servants. Such painstaking scholarship is now almost as dead as its authors; but such publications deserve to remain our living, albeit often primitive, models for reconstructing

---

[3] One exception is now available in *Écrit et Pouvoir dans les Chancelleries Médiévales: Espace Français, Espace Anglais*, ed. Kouky Fianu and DeLloyd J. Guth (Louvain-La-Neuve, 1997), especially for late medieval England's civil service in articles by D.A. Carpenter, W.M. Ormrod, A.L. Murray, C.J. Neville, T.S. Haskett, and the 'Introduction: Formulary and Literacy as Keys to Unlocking Late-Medieval Law' by DeLloyd J. Guth.

[4] T.F. Tout, *Chapters in the Administrative History of Medieval England: the Wardrobe, the Chamber, and the Small Seals* (6 vols, Manchester, 1920–33); W.H. Dunham, Jr, *The English Government at Work* (Cambridge, MA, 1940); N. Denholm-Young, *Seignorial Administration in England* (Oxford, 1937); S.B. Chrimes, *Introduction to the Administrative History of Medieval England* (Oxford, 1952); A.J. Otway-Ruthven, *The King's Secretary and the Signet Office of the XV Century* (Cambridge, 1939); R. Somerville, *History of the Duchy of Lancaster, 1265–1603* (London, 1953); A.B. Steel, *The Receipt of the Exchequer, 1377–1485* (Cambridge, 1954); B. Wilkinson, *The Chancery under Edward III* (Manchester, 1929); M. Hastings, *The Court of Common Pleas in Fifteenth-Century England* (Ithaca, N.Y., 1947); M. Blatcher, *The Court of King's Bench, 1450–1550* (London, 1978); and B.P. Wolffe, *The Crown Lands, 1461 to 1536* (London, 1970), and *The Royal Demesne in English History . . . to 1509* (London, 1971). Not one of these scholars directly addressed the mentality and reality of a civil service, but its activities can be understood by reading between their lines. Likewise, the numerous studies of patronage, in the K.B. McFarlane tradition, usually do not explicity or formally analyze what I have styled civil-service functions.

administrative, judicial and legislative business. Only the Selden Society's annual volumes since 1886 have sustained the institutional tradition to the present day, albeit with an increasing emphasis on lawyer's law. Any perusal of my 1976 *Late-medieval England* bibliography, alongside Joel Rosenthal's 1994 update, under the categories of political, constitutional, administrative and legal history, proves the point about neglect.[5] If we cannot improve on T.F. Tout's six volumes of soporific formalism, we can appreciate how far away we remain from understanding the institutions, royal and local, that required a civil service. As Elton amply proved for the sixteenth century, administrative history need not be boring and is essential for all studies of personnel and their institutional productivity.

As for the existence of a fifteenth-century civil service, the absence of archival material means the subject is often neglected: students of late medieval bureaucracy remain to be recruited. One exception is Ralph Griffiths, who at least raised the subject of 'public and private bureaucracies' almost twenty years ago. He did so alongside another essay, marking Gerald Aylmer's distinguished career commitment to studies of the early modern royal civil service.[6] Both articles have contributed to this essay's attempt to outline an accurate historical context for that late medieval pre-eminent civil servant, Sir Reynold Bray (*c.* 1440–1503).

Aylmer associated a civil service entirely with post-Restoration modernization, labelling what preceded it as mere 'office-holding'. Thus, the criteria for its existence became 'competitive entry examinations, grades, salaries, security of tenure, retirement pensions and the rest'. Aylmer offered this without the arrogance of presentism but, like Elton, he juxtaposed his chosen field of study at

---

[5] DeLloyd J. Guth, *Late-medieval England, 1377–1485* (Cambridge, 1976); 'Fifteenth-Century England: Recent Scholarship and Future Directions', *British Studies Monitor*, VII (1976–7), 3–50, in which I also did not raise the topic of a civil service; and J.T. Rosenthal, *Late Medieval England (1377–1485): A Bibliography of Historical Scholarship, 1975–1989* (Kalamazoo, 1994).

[6] G.E. Aylmer, 'From Office-Holding to Civil Service: The Genesis of Modern Bureaucracy', *Transactions of the Royal Historical Society*, 5th series, XXX (1980), 91–108; and R.A. Griffiths, 'Public and Private Bureaucracies in England and Wales in the Fifteenth Century', *Transactions of the Royal Historical Society*, 5th series, XXX (1980), 109–30.

the expense of its preceding period and culture. Thus, the 1660s to 1780s marked replacement of the 'old administrative system . . . alias the unreformed civil service'.[7] And what Elton did to the fifteenth century, on behalf of the Tudors, Aylmer did to the Tudors and Stuarts, on behalf of the Georgian era. Aylmer described the 'old' system of 'office-holding' as being in place from 'the end of the Middle Ages', with six characteristics: (1) entry to office by patronage, patrimony or purchase, and (2) by reversionary interest, venality and 'treatment of offices as if they were subject to normal rights of private property'; (3) tenure either for life or at pleasure; (4) carried out by deputy, encouraging absenteeism and sinecurism; (5) remuneration by fees, gratuities and perquisites, 'more than' by salaries, wages and stipends; and, (6) office-holding based on private right or interest 'rather than [as] a public service'.[8] His assertion, in (2) and (6), that an office approximated to the legal status of a proprietary right at common law must be superficially suspect, as must the total exclusion of competence and training from Aylmer's 'entry' criteria.

His characteristics of the 'old' system have become caricatures because he offered little or no primary evidence and no references to the earlier secondary scholarship on medieval administration, noted above. Aylmer would have benefitted greatly by using the next essay in the same volume of the *Transactions*. Ralph Griffiths there added primary narrative evidence to 'the medieval civil service' that T.F. Tout 'described'.[9]

Griffiths pointed out that the very word for 'bureaucracy' derived from the Old French, *burel*, meaning an official cloth covering administrative tables with computational squares for accounting purposes: hence a *bureau* with direct kinship to the English Exchequer's tablecloth. Griffiths's focus was on several dozen late medieval 'bureaucrats [who] were drawn from every class in society', educated in grammar schools, some at university and many at London's Inns, especially those of Chancery, and trained with the help of the plethora of

[7] Aylmer, 'From Office-Holding to Civil Service', pp. 92 and 102.

[8] *Ibid.*

[9] Griffiths, 'Public and Private Bureaucracies', p. 110.

vademecum business manuals and formulary copybooks. He agreed that most obtained employment and promotion by 'patronage, influence and "connection"', exemplified by letters of recommendation from the likes of the Pastons (which read rather like modern academic reference letters for one's own students!). The mobility of individuals in and out of 'public and private bureaucracies' was common. Hundreds of skilled men served 'church and state, crown and subject, city and estate', as receivers, counsellors, auditors and stewards, often on circuit for weeks at a time.[10] Griffiths exposed Aylmer's 'old' system as definitely personalized, creating both dependency and loyalty, but also as one where entry into office by patronage did not preclude priorities for merit and training, and where earnings were contractually fixed, monetary standards, and being based on a user-free principle. These were jobs requiring literacy and numeracy, if they were to be retained.

In late medieval England the idea of a 'civil service' remained broad in practice, not exclusively equated with royal service, and uniquely expressed in Middle English vocabulary and usage. The word 'service' universally characterized medieval society's personal relationships, as rooted in economic, class and political dependencies. 'Civil' would be juxtaposed against military, 'civilized' against barbaric, and in matters legal 'civil' would mean something that was not common law, not canon law, not customary law and not criminal pleadings. Its derivation from *civis*, meaning citizen, located it in the broad area of cultural urbanity and lawful polity. Conceptualization began there, in the etymology of *civis* as the opposite of a *peregrinus* (foreigner or stranger), but also with *civis* as the opposite of a *hostis* (a public enemy, to the *civitas* of each *civis*) and of an *inimicus* (a private enemy, to each *civis*).[11] Indeed, such a contemporary word study enables one to understand better what was at stake in those later fifteenth-century events that should be simply labelled civil wars, but which instead floridly became the Wars of the Roses.

[10] *Ibid.*, pp. 112, 116, 122.

[11] *Dictionary of Medieval Latin from British Sources: Fasicule II–C*, ed. R.W. Latham (London, 1981), at pp. 349–50, for 'civilis' and 'civis' and 'civiliter' and 'civitas'. The entries for 'communis' and 'communitas' are also vital, pp. 399–401.

Late medieval English routinely used 'ciuil' (also 'seuile' and 'ciwell') when referring to any political or secular authority, as in Reynold Pecock's noting that 'He kepith ye cyuyl lordschip in comoun with summe neizboris'. Contemporary with this is the Vegetius definition, rendered in Middle English as: 'Ciuile office, yat is to seye ye office of governayle of citees, townes, and contrees'. In medieval Latin, 'ciuilis' and 'ciuiliter' were like the Middle English 'ciuilitie' in meaning a public authority exercised by one's lord. Both languages in the fifteenth century used such words to focus on those offices and appointments associated with such services.[12]

If there was one Middle-English word that filled the mouths and minds of fifteenth-century humanity it most likely was 'seruise', and its variants: 'seruage', 'seruaunt', 'seruen', 'seruile' and 'seruitour'. From at least the thirteenth century, the noun 'seruaunt' meant simply 'one owing a duty of service to a master or lord', with first priority to God, Christ or the Virgin Mary. John Lydgate made clear that 'seruant or officer, in thyn office . . . to pore & riche doon pleyn iustice'. One could be said to 'seruen at the barre' as a lawyer or 'seruen to the citee', while 'somme seruen ye kyng and his siluer in cheker and in chancerye'. The verb 'seruen' specifically referred to service at a lord's court, as a retainer, and to the demand for one's obedience to commands and requests. In law the verb actively served writs and warrants, indictments and judgements. With non-personal subjects, 'seruen' identified a benefit, a vital function, as well as a sufficiency or satisfaction. At least eleven distinct usages existed for the noun 'servise', most immediately as synonymous with employment and more specifically as that which one performed in a lord's court and administration.[13]

There is no evidence of 'ciuil' and 'seruise' being used together in fifteenth-century vocabulary. Gerald Aylmer pointed out that 'the designation "civil servant" was slow to take hold even during the nineteenth century'.[14] To insist

[12] *Middle English Dictionary*, eds H. Kurath and S. Kuhn (Ann Arbor, 1959), Part C.1–D.5, at pp. 286–7, for 'civil' and 'civilian'.

[13] *Middle English Dictionary: S–SL*, ed. R.E. Lewis (Ann Arbor, 1986), 471–98, at pp. 473–6 for 'seruaunt', at pp. 477–87 for the verb 'seruen', and pp. 489–97 for 'seruise'.

[14] Aylmer, 'From Office-Holding to Civil Service', p. 91.

that historians only use the vocabulary available at the times and places studied is an absurdity. When we recognize late medieval words being used to describe functions familiar to modern culture, then certainly we must use modern vocabulary for modern readers. And when those functions clearly included public and community governance, we are still left with the historian's duty to document how the words operated institutionally and personally, as descriptive vessels containing particular types of human acts.

When put in context, the differences with our late twentieth-century world remain dramatic and instructive. Lawful polity grew in late medieval culture from a real property base, where the right to land brought both the right and duty to jurisdiction, which literally meant the right to speak, that is, to declare, the law as vested in the landlady or landlord for their particular parcel of land and for those on it. Those who administered the law acted in a civil capacity, indeed made a living serving as estate managers for the land-based civil orders, whether local gentry, substantial boroughs and cities, regional nobility, or the monarchy: acting as rent-gatherers, manorial court-holders, stewards, attorneys, deputy sheriffs and in a wide variety of other roles, usually as periodic circuit-riders, particularly during the four law terms. The prerequisites for each office holder were literacy, loyalty and the seal of legitimacy for their acts. Security of tenure in such service remained at the lord's or lady's pleasure, but was often secured mutually by oral or written contract. Most civil servants remained in horizontal rather than vertical advancement, moving to similar official functions with other employers. For the few who were lucky and able enough to use their civil-service skills to move upwards – in terms of status, income grants and responsibility – the rewards could be enormous, albeit so could the costs if the employer's fortunes failed. With that image and metaphor of a 'civil-service pole' in mind, one can find no better example of a successful fifteenth-century climber than Sir Reynold Bray.

Born most likely in the early 1440s in the parish of St John Bedwardine, Worcester, his parents had leased the manor of Laughern Beauchamp there in 1443 from Sir John Beauchamp of Powick, a cousin to Lady Margaret Beaufort. The link between the Bray and Beaufort families was present early on, if indirectly. Reynold's father, Richard Bray, had Northamptonshire origins and his mother, Joan Troughton, possibly came from the Guildford area of Surrey.

Reynold was their first-born, followed by John (the younger) and three daughters: Lucy, Alice and Joan. Reynold had an older half-brother, also named John, who was Richard's son by a first wife. The second John (the younger) served with Reynold, probably from their late teens, in the household of Sir Henry Stafford and his wife, Lady Margaret Beaufort. It was this brother, later John Bray of Eaton Braye, Bedfordshire, who ultimately provided the apparently childless Reynold with a nephew and male heir, Edmund, when he died in 1503.[15]

By 1465, Reynold had acquitted himself well enough in the Stafford household to be named their receiver-general. He worked as rent-collector in the Somerset area and his brother John did the same in Westmorland. John also moved messages and moneys regularly, usually from Stafford residences in London and Woking, while keeping his own residence in Worcester. He did not accompany Sir Henry Stafford in his retinue through the south-west and the Welsh Marches in the autumn of 1467 or again in March 1470, supporting Edward IV in Lincolnshire and at York. John's service remained more strictly limited to estate administration under Reynold's direction. Unlike Reynold, John acted as an employee, not a personal retainer, and when Sir Henry died in 1471 John Bray did not follow his older brother in serving the widow when she soon married her third husband, Thomas, Lord Stanley. Her three seriatim marriages would bring an accumulation of landed estates which enhanced Reynold Bray's entire adult life. His career, friendships, family connections and prosperity as a landlord in his own right ultimately transcended and fulfilled his civil-service career when he became an administrator to the biggest collection of estates, the English realm of King Henry VII.

It was Lady Margaret's first marriage at the age of fourteen that had produced the most significant focal point for Reynold's civil service.[16] In 1455 Henry VI's

[15] M.M. Condon, 'Sir Reynold Bray (d. 1503)', forthcoming in the *New Dictionary of National Biography*; DeLloyd J. Guth, 'Sir Reginald [*sic*] Bray: "Not He That Made the Smoke"', *Report of the Society of the Friends of St. George's and the Descendants of the Knights of the Garter*, ed. M.H. Bond, V (1970–1), 67–73.

[16] M.K. Jones and M.G. Underwood, *The King's Mother: Lady Margaret Beaufort, Countess of Richmond and Derby* (Cambridge, 1992).

government had pre-empted her Beaufort and Beauchamp fortunes (which came to her as an orphaned three-year-old when her father John Beaufort, the duke of Somerset, died in 1444), by marrying her to Edmund Tudor, earl of Richmond, eldest son of Owen Tudor and Katherine de Valois, Henry V's widow. As countess of Richmond, married to Henry VI's half-brother, she soon created even greater pre-eminence through her son, Henry Tudor, born at Pembroke Castle on 28 January 1457, she having been widowed two months earlier. Her second marriage to Stafford further cemented the Lancastrian identity, as did the protection of Jasper Tudor. After the small bloodbath at Towton on 29 March 1461, the Staffords themselves showed political flexibility and respect for continuity, as they began to embrace Edward IV's new Yorkist order. The new king and Sir William Herbert had secured Lady Margaret's five-year-old son, removing him from Pembroke Castle to Herbert's wardship in Raglan Castle. By 1465, in this well-known narrative, Reynold Bray began to document his civil service to Lady Margaret.

We have various holograph notebooks for 1467–9 and 1474–5, supplemented by Stafford household accounts surviving from 1465.[17] In two of them, now in Westminster Abbey's Muniments Room, we see Bray keeping a day-book of duties. Beyond mere money-gathering, he acted as agent for Sir Henry and Lady Margaret separately and jointly, in a steady stream of property litigation necessary to defend and extend their respective estates. Within their vast and scattered jurisdictions were diverse local communities, each presenting countless needs for supervision, arbitration and control among the tenants' interests. We do not know if Bray had formal legal training, but if so it would probably have been at an Inn of Chancery in London. He routinely convened Lady Margaret's manorial courts, adjudicated tenants' disputes and enforced local customs, against such public nuisances as gossiping and profiteering. He provides an excellent insight into what mattered to such a civil servant: details about diet, prices, wages, transport, itineraries, fees, litigation costs and the networks of

---

[17] Westminster Abbey Muniments, MS 5472, MS 5472,* and MS 5479.**

persons in and out of the Stafford household. Bray was a 'master fixer': someone who learned and preferred to use the system of civil order, with its interpersonal networks, to resolve, stall and avoid conflicts without resorting to physical confrontations, force, violence and ultimately war.

Margaret Condon has abundantly documented the post-1485 'profits of office' aspect of Bray's later career, where his pre-1485 civil service appears as an apprenticeship to post-Bosworth crown service.[18] Her primary sources for this are land transaction records (for example, *de banco* rolls, feet of fines, close rolls) in the Public Record Office, and they reveal how Bray exemplified after 1485 the eternal verity that 'the profit of office and power was visible wealth'. But that was at the end of his life and story. Regardless of what Bray ended up with, and most civil servants like him were nowhere near as lucratively successful, it was his professionalism that has told us more about fifteenth-century order, stability and security. After 1485, Bray effectively became Henry VII's central estate administrator, for a king who increasingly treated the whole of England and Wales in such metaphorical and material terms.

Bray was in no way unique in the fifteenth century as someone who actually did what civil offices required, whether in private or public service, to borrow Ralph Griffiths's 1980 distinction. But this distinction may not clarify the realities of a fifteenth-century world that also roughly distinguished, but did not separate, the universalizing of law from the particularizing of administration. Bray was an administrator, not a lawyer. This centrifugally inward versus centripetally outward motion and metaphor also captured vivacious distinctions between a universalizing Church and a secularised self-interest, between national identity (as Englishness, and certainly as Welshness!) and local affinity, and between crown-controlled, politically based law and order and private property-based rights of self-governance.

Bray's pre-1485 civil service fell entirely on the side of the ledger identified with administration, not law; with promoting secular, not spiritual interests;

---

[18] M.M. Condon, 'From Caitiff and Villain to Pater Patriae: Reynold Bray and the Profits of Office', in *Profit, Piety and the Professions in Later Medieval England*, ed. Michael Hicks (Gloucester, 1990), pp. 137–68.

representing local family networks, not an abstracted nationalism; and working daily in a pluralism of competitive land-owning polities, not in the mono-tracked, mono-polity (that is, mono-poly) of monarchic, centralizing power. It is easy to see why he helped Henry VII to a vision that equated the realm with an estate, needing tight administration. In his crown service after 1485 Bray actually, apparently obsessively, performed his major offices: chancellor of the duchy of Lancaster, 'president' of the Royal Council, periodically as lord treasurer. Bray exercised all such senior posts in person, not through deputies, as many contemporary clients and associates did. At a second level, he became Henry VII's ubiquitous steward, dozens of times over, for royally administered lands acquired by inheritance, forfeiture, wardship, recoveries, escheat, etc. Often he delegated or even re-granted such offices, but there could be no doubt then and now that Bray remained in charge. And again we are reminded of his roots in the Wars of the Roses era, from the 1460s onwards, and of those holograph notebooks indicating a learned, highly personal type of accountability: to the Staffords, to the Stanleys and then to Henry VII.

In such civil-service experience there are signs of another theme, where the pragmatism of the administrative mind clashes with more strictly legal perspectives. By the mid-fifteenth century, law *per se* was in retreat to equity, as practised in the court of Chancery and then under Henry VII in conciliar courts of Star Chamber, Requests and in the chancellorship of the duchy of Lancaster.[19] Other than Chancery, Bray played the central role from 1485 to 1503 in these conciliar and duchy jurisdictions. In place of law-resolving for disputes, as in the common law courts of King's Bench, Common Pleas and Exchequer, with their ossifying cultures of fixed and expensive writ processes and lawyers, equity resolving offered a pragmatic process born of administrative minds, guided by highly personalized priorities for making decisions and by invoking a vocabulary of 'fairness', 'equitable', 'reasonableness', 'common sense' and 'justice'. Equity

---

[19] J.H. Baker, *An Introduction to English Legal History* (London, 1990, 3rd edn), esp. chs III, VI, and VII; DeLloyd J. Guth, 'Enforcing Late-Medieval Law: Patterns in Litigation during Henry VII's Reign', in *Legal Records and the Historian*, ed. J.H. Baker (London, 1978), pp. 80–96.

process resolved disputes on the basis of fact, not law, according to discretion rather than rules, allowing a judge's conscience to determine rights and wrongs, thereby avoiding legal formalism and a tyranny of rules.

Such courts of conscience blossomed in the second half of the century, under Yorkists and Lancastrians, because common-law process increasingly became identified as slow, technical, land based, often corrupt and out-of-touch for a variety of practical needs, such as in copyhold tenure, enfeoffments to uses and non-feasant contracts. What equity championed was precisely what Bray practised before 1485, namely that individual conscience and local landlord customs were preferred sources for norms by which conflicts should be resolved. In his constant travels as an estate manager, specifically in holding routine manorial courts, he would have applied measures that did not rest on the authority of learned lawyers and judges in Westminster Hall. In the time-honoured tradition of service to masters and clients, one's first purpose was to keep them out of such law courts.

How can we know Bray as administrator and as equitable adjudicator? I have already noted that Bray's notebooks survive from the dark days of civil war, to reveal daily duties undertaken to govern tenants and local jurisdictions. They are in the muniments that came to Westminster Abbey on the death of Bray's patroness, Lady Margaret Beaufort, six years after his death. But even more interesting, at least to a legal and administrative historian, are letters written to him at the peak of his royal service. These reveal the wide extent to which a highly personalized, discretionary power was seen to be vested in Bray, in the name of the king.

The Bray letters in Westminster Abbey can probably be dated to about 1502.[20] Because all lack any regnal or Christian year, we have had to resort to intensive content and context analyses, as well as to the watermarks in the paper. They are mainly in the form of petitions personally addressed to Bray, although some are reports prompted by Bray's prior requests for information. They may even have come from Bray's in-tray, perhaps his last, related to work within Henry VII's

---

[20] Westminster Abbey Muniments, MSS 16016–16080.

unique 'council learned in the laws'. The petitions ring with that vocabulary of equity: that credence, fairness, reasonableness should prevail, regarding a sought-after decision in a formalized dispute, a patronage position, a property transaction or a waiver of crown rights. Like Thomas More, a later chancellor of the duchy, Bray was asked to intervene in every conceivable type of self-interested local matter of governance. His range of topics was breathtakingly broad: letters pertain to performance of a will, a riot led by a Wiltshire landlord, an audit of a deceased royal servant's goods, a wardship, purchases of lands, nominations to religious confraternities, Bray's intervention in a murder case, confidential information about evasions of royal revenue rights, management matters on his own estates, the building of Bath Abbey and all sorts of patronage requests. Here we see the administrative and the equity roles working in the one person, to protect and promote the royal interest. With Bray's death in 1503, such matters and powers fell, or divided, to Richard Empson and Edmund Dudley.[21] Unlike Bray, they did not die in bed, but like him, they could be called civil servants. The evidence of Bray from 1502 tentatively suggests that the system attributed to Empson-Dudley was already in place, with its relocating of power and priority and administrative and discretionary experience, placing decision making outside common law and due process. It may even point to Bray as that régime's architect and prime administrator. As Margaret Condon has already shown, he certainly reaped that régime's rewards. But such speculatory explanations, revisionary for the entire reign, must await completion of our jointly edited 'Bray letters' project.

If we turn away from that petitionary, greed-seeking, self-promoting world of the Bray letters, all written by others to him, to his civil-service notebooks compiled thirty-five years earlier, amid hundreds of legal and management memorabilia, we find hints of an avuncular relationship between Bray and Lady Margaret's young lad. In 1467 Bray noted several trips made to Raglan Castle to the thirteen-year-old earl of Richmond, bearing 'messages' and 'Tythynges'

---

[21] This civil-service perspective can enhance one's re-reading of *The Tree of Commonwealth: A Treatise Written by Edmund Dudley*, ed. D.M. Brodie (Cambridge, 1948).

(tidings), and money; and then in 1469 'delivered to my lord Richemond at Webley for his disportes to bie hym bowe and Shaftes'.[22] Neither could have known the extent to which the lad would need familiarity with such basic weapons of war sixteen years later, at the age of twenty-nine, on his march from Milford Haven to Market Bosworth.

This last notebook ended in 1470 with Bray writing, without details or examples, about 'Trouble in the World', as Henry VI and his supporters began their short-lived Lancastrian interruption of the Yorkist monarchy. Fifteen years later, Sir Reynold and his newly crowned king would launch their own régime for solving, or at least controlling, any further 'Trouble in the World'. At its heart, for better and worse, Henry VII's régime would prove how much a civil-service mentality and reality mattered. Once we document and understand this, we begin to know better who were the enduring winners at Bosworth.

---

[22] Westminster Abbey Muniments, MS 5472, ff. 44r–45r.

4

LAWRENCE BOOTH: BISHOP OF DURHAM (1457–76), ARCHBISHOP OF YORK (1476–80)

A. Compton Reeves

When John Booth of Barton-upon-Irwell, Lancashire, died in 1422 he could have had no inkling that two of his sons would become archbishops, nor that his descendants over several generations would have an impressive impact upon the English Church. The first son to enter the episcopate was William, who became bishop of Coventry and Lichfield (1447–52) and then archbishop of York (1452–64). A decade after William became a bishop, another son, Lawrence, became bishop of Durham (1457–76), and a dozen years after William's death became himself archbishop of York (1476–80). A grandson of John Booth, another John, was bishop of Exeter (1465–78), while a great-grandson, Charles, was bishop of Hereford (1516–35), and there were numerous other Booths and Booth kinsmen who were also dignitaries of the late medieval English Church.

The member of the Booth family who is the focus of this essay is Lawrence, the second of the Booth archbishops of York. As Lawrence pursued his ecclesiastical career, he clearly benefited by following the pioneering lead of William, who obtained specialized education in the common law at Gray's Inn and began accumulating ecclesiastical benefices in 1420 when he took clerical orders. Who might have aided William in his early ecclesiastical career as he shifted from the common law remains a mystery, but a potentially viable candidate as patron is his fellow Lancashireman, Thomas Langley, who was in 1420 both bishop of Durham and chancellor of England.[1] William Booth was

---

[1] For Langley, see R.L. Storey, *Thomas Langley and the Bishopric of Durham, 1406–1437* (London, 1961).

obviously a man of ability, and in the 1440s he attracted the powerful patronage of the duke of Suffolk and of Queen Margaret of Anjou, whose household chancellor he became. Lawrence, whose life history indicates that he was perhaps some twenty or more years younger than William, acquired an academic education in civil law at Cambridge University, which he later served as chancellor. Lawrence was ordained as a priest in 1446, a quarter of a century after William's ordination, and it was assuredly helpful to Lawrence as he developed his ecclesiastical career that William was in a position to act as his mentor.[2] Lawrence, for instance, like William, served Queen Margaret as chancellor. Lawrence not only confirmed the ecclesiastical and administrative career paradigm for talented members of his family as initiated by William, but he also carried that career paradigm to its greatest heights by virtue of becoming not only an archbishop in the English Church, but also through royal secular service as keeper of the privy seal under King Henry VI and chancellor of England under King Edward IV.

It is important to examine the early foundations of Lawrence's successful public career. An early action by Lawrence in his pursuit of an ecclesiastical career was to reconcile a misstep of his parents. William Booth was a son of John Booth and his wife Joan, daughter of Sir Henry Trafford of Trafford, Lancashire. Lawrence, however, was the son of John Booth and an unknown woman to whom he was not married. In 1442 Lawrence obtained a papal dispensation which authorized him to hold multiple benefices with or without cure of souls. It was also mentioned therein that Lawrence had already been dispensed for promotion to holy orders even though he was the son of unmarried parents and dispensed as well to hold two benefices simultaneously.[3] The earlier papal dispensation for bastardy is lost, but it must be dated no later than January 1440, for in that month Lawrence became rector of the Church of St Mary Magdalen, Milk Street, London, a benefice he exchanged in December 1441 for the rectory of

---

[2] A.B. Emden, *A Biographical Register of the University of Cambridge to 1500* (Cambridge, 1963), p. 78; A.C. Reeves, *Lancastrian Englishmen* (Washington, D.C., 1981), pp. 265–6.

[3] *C[alendar of] P[apal] L[etters] (1431–47)*, pp. 258–9.

St Botolph's, London (which he vacated by exchange in 1445).[4] That the first recorded ecclesiastical benefice of Lawrence Booth was in the diocese of London suggests the influence of William Booth. In 1421, by the patronage of Henry V (the diocese of London being without a bishop at the time), William Booth gained the modest prebend of Consumpta-per-Mare and a place in the cathedral chapter of St Paul's, London.[5] Over the following years, by financial acumen and administrative skill, William consolidated the management of the chapter's resources and augmented his control over them. He was well placed in the diocese of London by 1440 to give a push to Lawrence's career, and it is not unreasonable to suppose that he did so.

Once Lawrence had begun the process, he moved ahead with his quest for benefices. For less than a year, from mid-1444 into early 1445, he held the prebend of Gaia Major in the diocese of Coventry and Lichfield, where William would become bishop in 1447.[6] Also in 1444 Lawrence became rector of Hemingford Abbots in Huntingtonshire, and did not vacate this benefice until 1448.[7] In March 1445 he obtained the rectory of All Saints, Cottenham, Cambridgeshire (which he retained until December 1456), and this benefice is appropriately associated with Lawrence's academic training in the civil law at Cambridge University.[8] Whereas William Booth was trained in English common law, Lawrence chose civil law and began a long association between the Booth family and Cambridge. A papal dispensation was issued to Lawrence early in 1448, addressing him as rector of Cottenham and as bachelor of laws, allowing him to hold simultaneously any number of mutually compatible benefices and

[4] Emden, *Cambridge*, p. 78. A summary of Booth's life, with an account of his benefices, is A.H. Thompson, 'Laurence Booth', in *Dictionnaire d'Histoire et de Géographie Ecclésiastiques* (Paris, 1937), 9, 1164–6.

[5] C.N.L. Brooke, 'The Earliest Times to 1485', in W.R. Matthews and W.M. Atkins (eds), *A History of St Paul's Cathedral* (London, 1957), pp. 63, 91.

[6] John Le Neve, *Fasti Ecclesiae Anglicanae, 1300–1541, X, Coventry and Lichfield Diocese*, compiled by B. Jones (London, 1964), p. 41.

[7] Emden, *Cambridge*, p. 78.

[8] *Ibid.*

relieving him of mentioning his illegitimacy in any future official dealings with the papacy; in November 1450 a papal dispensation, addressing him as licentiate of laws, authorized Lawrence to hold two incompatible benefices.[9] Meanwhile, in 1446, Lawrence had become canon of Stoke by Clare, Suffolk, and a prebendary of Norwich Cathedral, a benefice he held until at least 1454.[10]

The year 1450 provides many details of how Lawrence's ecclesiastical career was progressing. He had completed his formal academic training, and had begun what would be a lifelong term as master of Pembroke College, Cambridge, where he had become a fellow in 1447.[11] Brother William Booth had become bishop of Coventry and Lichfield, but the collapse in 1450 of the government of the duke of Suffolk, with which he was associated, made his position uncertain for a time, and his life was threatened in the rebellion of Jack Cade later in the same year.[12] Early in the year a licence was obtained under the leadership of Bishop William for the foundation of a chantry dedicated to St Katherine in the family's home parish church of St Mary the Virgin, Eccles, Lancashire.[13] William was joined in the foundation of the chantry by his brothers Thomas (the eldest), Robert, John and Roger, by his sisters Margery, Elizabeth, Katherine, Joan and Alice, by his five brothers-in-law and assorted nephews, and by his clerical kinsmen, Lawrence and Richard Booth and Seth Worsley, treasurer of Lichfield.[14] William Booth's parents, together with the king and queen, were to benefit from the prayers of the two chaplains supported by the endowment of the chantry. In 1456, Lawrence Booth and three kinsmen added to the chantry endowment with the gift of the advowson of the church of Slaidburn, Yorkshire.[15] The inclusion of Lawrence in the foundation of the chantry of St Katherine, and his further endowing of that

---

[9] *C.P.L. (1447–55)*, pp. 338, 516.

[10] Emden, *Cambridge*, pp. 78–9.

[11] *Ibid.*, p. 78.

[12] Reeves, *Lancastrian Englishmen*, pp. 282–3.

[13] C[alendar of] P[atent] R[olls] *(1446–52)*, p. 322. See also *C.P.L. (1458–71)*, pp. 258–67.

[14] F.R. Raines, *A History of the Chantries within the County of Lancaster* (2 vols, Chetham Society, 59–60, 1862), 1, 131–5; Reeves, *Lancastrian Englishmen*, pp. 276–9.

[15] *C.P.R. (1452–61)*, p. 275.

project, clearly suggest a sense of identity with the Booth family that was in no way weakened, but may perhaps have been made more tenacious, by the fact that his parents were not married. By 1450, Lawrence seems to have been comfortably supported by ecclesiastical benefices. In addition to the benefices previously mentioned, he had been collated in June 1449 by Bishop William to the prebend of Offley and a canonry in Lichfield Cathedral, and five months later he exchanged Offley for the prebend of Oxgate in the diocese of London.[16] William Booth would necessarily have ceased to be a member of the cathedral chapter of St Paul's upon his elevation to the episcopate, but his ties and influence there cannot have entirely disappeared, and he may have played some part in Lawrence's exchange of Offley for Oxgate. Lawrence was now a canon of St Paul's and moving in an environment thoroughly familiar to his half-brother, and later events indicate that Lawrence made the best of his opportunities.

Like William, Lawrence was to remain a member of the cathedral chapter of St Paul's until he became a bishop, and it gave to both men a visible presence in the geographical heart of political power. Lawrence remained prebendary of Oxgate from November 1449 until 21 November 1453, when he became prebendary of Weldland, and on the very same day he resigned Weldland to become prebendary of Mapesbury. He held this prebend until 25 November 1456 when he gave up Mapesbury for the prebend of Totenhall, an exchange which came just three days after Lawrence had been elected dean of St Paul's and thus head of the cathedral chapter.[17]

Lawrence had scrambled in a few short years to the highest dignity in the cathedral chapter of St Paul's, but his benefice garnering had not been limited to the diocese of London. Briefly in 1452 Booth again held the prebend of Offley in Lichfield Cathedral, which he exchanged for the prebend of Tervin in the same cathedral church, and he kept Tervin until he became a bishop.[18] Between 1452

---

[16] Le Neve, *Fasti*, X, 48. Booth would hold Offley again for a few months in 1452.

[17] John Le Neve, *Fasti Ecclesiae Anglicanae, 1300–1541*, V. *St Paul's, London*, compiled by J.M. Horn (London, 1963), pp. 53, 67, 46, 63, 6.

[18] Le Neve, *Fasti*, X, 48, 60; *C.P.R. (1452–61)*, p. 28.

and 1457 he was a canon of the collegiate church of Beverley in Yorkshire.[19] In 1452 Lawrence was serving as chancellor for Margaret of Anjou, queen of Henry VI, and, as it happened, the temporalities of the bishopric of Lincoln were in the hands of the king, who bestowed the archdeaconry of Stowe in Lincoln diocese upon Booth on 10 April.[20] He remained archdeacon of Stowe for only a few months, and then resigned in favour of a young kinsman, Edmund Booth, who went on to become a Cambridge University bachelor of canon law and another Booth member of the cathedral chapter of St Paul's before his death in 1456.[21] Once again it is possible to observe a manifestation of the family career paradigm of law, church, administration and mentoring by kinsmen.

During his brief tenure as archdeacon of Stowe and, doubtless more importantly, while in the service of Queen Margaret, Lawrence obtained papal permission to employ a deputy to carry out his archidiaconal duties, to hold additional incompatible benefices, and to farm all the benefices he held.[22] If plans were being implemented in 1452 to free his time from attention to his benefices so that his talents could be utilized by the government, the pope, the university, his older half-brother or something else, nothing immediately developed. He did in 1452 obtain as an additional benefice the vicarage of Holy Trinity, Coventry.[23] It was in 1452 that William Booth took up the post of archbishop of York, and in the next year Lawrence became a canon of York and prebendary of Wistow.[24] He retained the prebend of Wistow until a few months before becoming a bishop, when he was replaced by his nephew, John Booth, the future bishop of Exeter.[25] Between vacating Wistow and becoming a bishop,

---

[19] Emden, *Cambridge*, p. 79.

[20] *C.P.R. (1446–52)*, p. 527; John Le Neve, *Fasti Ecclesiae Anglicanae, 1300–1541*, I. *Lincoln Diocese*, compiled by H.P.F. King (London, 1962), p. 19.

[21] Emden, *Cambridge*, p. 77.

[22] *C.P.L. (1447–55)*, pp. 120, 125–6, 129, 241.

[23] Emden, *Cambridge*, p. 79.

[24] John Le Neve, *Fasti Ecclesiae Anglicanae, 1300–1541*, VI. *Northern Province*, compiled by B. Jones (London, 1963), p. 93.

[25] *Ibid.*, VI, 94.

Lawrence held the prebend of Wetwang and thereby remained a canon of York.[26] Incidentally, the prebend of Wistow would later be held in turn by Robert Clifton (1479–1500) and by Gamalial Clifton (1500–41), both of whom were Booth kinsmen.[27] As archbishop of York, Lawrence would, in 1478, bestow the prebend of Wetwang upon a fellow kinsman of illegitimate birth, Robert Booth.[28] Robert studied at Cambridge, but his doctorate in civil law may have come from a non-English university, and he was prebendary of Wetwang until his death in 1488. Thanks to William Booth, Lawrence was archdeacon of Richmond in the archdiocese of York from 1454 until 1457, and briefly in 1457 Lawrence was provost of Beverley in Yorkshire.[29] Having completed a survey of Lawrence's pre-episcopal collecting of benefices, his progress can be viewed as an informative example of a successful cleric on the upward climb toward a bishopric who utilized his skills as an administrator, his specialized education in law and his patronage connections, both within and beyond his family. Some additional matters must be considered, however, in order to present a more complete picture of Lawrence's career.

It will be recalled that Lawrence was for a time, beginning on 7 March 1451 in succession to his brother William, the household chancellor of Queen Margaret of Anjou.[30] The one financial account to survive from the household of Queen Margaret, for the fiscal year 1452–3, was produced during the period when Lawrence was directing the queen's chancery and was responsible for her great seal.[31] The chancellorship afforded opportunities of providing managerial service in circumstances where diligent labour and a display of talent could potentially

[26] *Ibid.*, VI, 91.

[27] *Ibid.*, VI, 94.

[28] Emden, *Cambridge*, pp. 79–80.

[29] *Ibid.*, p. 79; Le Neve, *Fasti*, VI, 26. Booth's register of acts as archdeacon of Richmond has been edited: A.H. Thompson, 'The Registers of the Archdeaconry of Richmond, 1361–1442', *Yorkshire Archaeological Journal*, 25 (1920), 112–20.

[30] Robert Somerville, *History of the Duchy of Lancaster* (2 vols, London, 1953–70), 1, 209.

[31] A.R. Myers, 'The Household of Queen Margaret of Anjou, 1452–3', *Bulletin of the John Rylands Library*, 40 (1957–8), 79–113, 391–431.

result in promotion to more prestigious posts, and it also carried the comfortable salary of £40 per annum, together with an annual £10 for his household. How long Lawrence carried out his secular responsibilities for Queen Margaret is not known, but his subsequent promotions suggest that his work was entirely satisfactory. He was, as we have seen, developing the ecclesiastical component of his career at the same time. He was also of sufficient standing to act as a feoffee in various legal arrangements concerning land.[32]

A grand promotion came on 24 September 1456 when Lawrence was named keeper of the privy seal of King Henry VI.[33] Less than two months later he became dean of St Paul's. Booth would hold the keepership of the privy seal until July 1460, and be the only member of his family to hold the office. In the appropriately descriptive words of Professor Brown, 'The keeper was a great officer of state, usually a university graduate with administrative or legal experience, looking forward to a bishopric.'[34] As keeper, Booth was head of one of the three great departments of the government. Documents authenticated by the privy seal were used for communications between the English government and foreign powers, for dispatching warrants from the king to the Chancery, ordering the issue of formal letters by the Chancery under the king's great seal, and directing warrants to the Exchequer, the third major department of government, for the issuing of payments. Booth as keeper had a place on the king's Council, and the privy seal was also used to initiate administrative action upon decisions of the king's Council, which did not obtain its own seal until 1556. Booth attended some sessions of the Council over the next few years, but not all.[35] William Booth, as archbishop of York, also had a place on the Council.

---

[32] C[alendar of] C[lose] R[olls] (1447–54), pp. 335, 484, 495; *ibid. (1452–61)*, p. 244.

[33] E.B. Fryde, D.E. Greenway, S. Porter and I. Roy (eds), *Handbook of British Chronology* (3rd edn, London, 1986), p. 95.

[34] A.L. Brown, 'The Privy Seal Clerks in the Early Fifteenth Century', in D.A. Bullough and R.L. Storey (eds), *The Study of Medieval Records: Essays in Honour of Kathleen Major* (Oxford, 1971), p. 273 n. 1.

[35] Roger Virgoe, 'The Composition of the King's Council', *Bulletin of the Institute of Historical Research*, 43 (1970), 159.

The half-brothers Booth were now truly eminent figures in the kingdom. In January 1457 the two Booths were among eleven lords, ecclesiastics and knights appointed to be councillors to the three-year-old Edward, prince of Wales.[36] Perhaps at about this time, and certainly by February 1457, Lawrence was chancellor of Cambridge University, a position he continued to hold at least until the end of 1458.[37] Booth was chancellor at the time the statutes were being confirmed for Henry VI's foundations of King's College, Cambridge, and Eton College.

To appreciate fully these dramatic advances in the career of Lawrence Booth they must be considered against the background of political events in the kingdom. King Henry VI had, in August 1453, slipped into an incapacitating mental state, and in the following October the royal heir, Prince Edward, was born. Imperative concerns for the safety of the ruling dynasty and the stability of the government were forced upon Queen Margaret, and she was a strong-willed woman who was not disposed to distancing herself from events unfolding. In spite of Margaret's opposition, Duke Richard of York, the premier critic in his day of the Lancastrian régime, in March 1454 became protector of England. York had a potential claim to the English throne, and Margaret rightly saw him as a threat to the regal future of her son. King Henry, however, recovered from his illness at about Christmas 1454, and shortly thereafter York's protectorate ended. There then ensued an anti-York political shift which made York and his allies anxious and suspicious of real or imagined political enemies. The tense political atmosphere was not ameliorated by negotiations, but instead degenerated into a clash of arms at St Albans on 22 May 1455 from which York emerged victorious. York's great rival, the duke of Somerset, was killed in the fighting, and he could conveniently be given posthumous blame for the recourse to arms. The events at St Albans in no way reconciled Margaret, Henry VI and their supporters to York. A second period of illness for Henry VI, perhaps physical in this instance rather than mental, led to a second York protectorate from November 1455 to

---

[36] *C.P.R. (1452–61)*, p. 359.
[37] *Ibid. (1452–61)*, p. 356; Emden, *Cambridge*, p. 78.

the following February. An eerie, surface calm, which endured for the next few years, settled over a political commmunity shocked by the violence of the clash at St Albans. The divisions of antipathy in the body politic were deep, and few leaders in public life seemed inclined to build bridges of reconciliation.

The Booth experience in this period exemplifies Queen Margaret's efforts to consolidate her support. William, a former household chancellor, remained archbishop of York and a royal councillor, and Lawrence, who had also served Margaret as chancellor, was appointed keeper of the privy seal and a royal councillor, and both men were members of the council of the young prince of Wales. When Robert Neville, bishop of Durham and a member of a family staunchly supportive of the duke of York, died in July 1457, the man whom Pope Calixtus III provided to the vacant see on 22 August was Lawrence Booth.[38] Two of the three sees of the northern province of the English Church were now occupied by Booths. Lawrence made his profession of obedience to the archbishop of York on 18 September and secured the spiritualities of the see on the same day. His consecration as bishop of Durham took place on 25 September at Sherburn-in-Elmet, Yorkshire, and the temporalities of the see were delivered into his custody on 18 October.[39] Lawrence would be bishop of Durham for nineteen years.

The Neville family, of whom the late bishop of Durham was one, was opposed by Queen Margaret, who was perhaps less than distraught at the passing from the scene of the ecclesiastic-brother of Richard Neville, earl of Salisbury, and the hand of Queen Margaret must be seen in the appointment of her household chancellor to the see of Durham as she sought to assert Lancastrian power against Neville and Yorkist influence in the diocese of Durham. Professor Storey

[38] Le Neve, *Fasti*, VI, 108–9.

[39] Between the day of Bishop Neville's death and the delivery of the temporalities to Bishop Booth no documents were issued from the diocesan chancery, no diocesan court sessions were held and no other official business was transacted because the king did not appoint anyone to have custody of a seal of vacancy for the bishopric. L.O. Pike and J. Burtt (eds), 'Durham Records: Calendar of the Cursitor's Records: Chancery Enrolments', in *The Thirty-Fifth Annual Report of the Deputy Keeper of the Public Records* (London, 1874), p. 79, hereafter cited as *35th DKR*.

sees Booth's accession as a 'serious blow' to Salisbury's power, but Professor Pollard notes examples of Booth's conciliatory approach and the continuance of a degree of Neville influence in the diocese after 1457, although the Neville influence was steadily diminished there. It had come to an exceedingly low ebb by 1459 through the attainder of Salisbury and his removal, together with that of his brother William Neville, Lord Fauconberg, from the judicial bench, and also through Booth's confiscation of the lordship of Barnard Castle, within the liberty of Durham, from Richard Neville, earl of Warwick, who is so well remembered as the 'Kingmaker'.[40] The Neville factor is important to keep in mind, as is the distinctly political side of Booth's appointment to Durham. This is not to imply, however, that any man in Booth's era who became a bishop was not expected to have political talent among his qualifications.

The diocese of Durham required a bishop possessed of administrative skills of a high order, for the diocese encompassed the county of Durham and lands in Northumberland and it lay on the border with Scotland.[41] That is not to say that the bishop of Durham (or any other bishop, for that matter) needed to administer his diocese personally, for there was in place a staff of officers who could carry on diocesan administration even in the absence of the bishop himself. To carry out the duties that only a bishop could undertake, a suffragan bishop was normally available. Secretarial and archival work was supervised by the bishop's registrar, the chancellor provided the bishop with legal counsel, an official presided over the bishop's court, and there was an archdeacon for each of the archdeaconries into which the diocese was subdivided, representing the counties of Durham and Northumberland. These were, moreover, only a few of the men in the service of the bishop.

Any discussion of Booth as bishop during the nearly two decades of his tenure as bishop of Durham is made very difficult by the loss of the register of Booth's

[40] R.L. Storey, *The End of the House of Lancaster* (London, 1966), p. 183; A.J. Pollard, *North-Eastern England During the Wars of the Roses* (Oxford, 1990), pp. 267–68, 274.

[41] For a description of the diocese earlier in the fifteenth century, see Storey, *Thomas Langley*, ch. IV.

official acts as bishop.[42] One matter of interest that can be noted, however, is the overwhelming likelihood that Bishop Booth was responsible for the appointment to the position of archdeacon of Durham of Ralph Booth, a son of Lawrence's half-brother, Roger Booth of Barton, and a canon law graduate of Cambridge who died in 1497.[43]

Booth's early years as bishop of Durham were a period of political upheaval in the realm. In 1459 the tension between the ruling house of Lancaster and the supporters of the opposing house of York erupted again into military conflict. An indecisive clash took place at Blore Heath in Staffordshire on 23 September as Queen Margaret sought to crush her enemies, but the duke of York and his followers regrouped to the west at Ludlow, where they were confronted by a royalist army. Some of York's followers drifted away, unwilling to confront the larger army of their king in battle, but a fight took place at Ludford Bridge, south of Ludlow, on the River Teme on 13 October which was a rout for the supporters of York. York himself and his second son, Earl Edmund of Rutland, fled to Ireland. York's eldest son, Earl Edward of March, and the earl of Warwick escaped to Calais. Some of the king's prominent opponents, Edward of March, Earl Richard of Warwick, and his father, Richard Neville, earl of Salisbury, led an invasion of south-eastern England in June 1460. They came up against the king's army at Northampton on 10 July, and after a short clash were triumphant, even capturing King Henry VI. Less than three weeks after the battle of Northampton, Lawrence Booth was replaced by Robert Stillington (whom Lawrence Booth would later replace as chancellor) as keeper of the privy seal.

Also in the aftermath of the battle of Northampton, York returned from Ireland and made a bid, in the forum of Parliament, to become king on the basis of his descent from King Edward III. The matter was too fraught with tension and partisan interests to be settled peacefully, and again there was

---

[42] It is possible to explore the nature of a Durham bishop's register from a few decades before Booth's time in R.L. Storey (ed.), *The Register of Thomas Langley, Bishop of Durham* (6 vols, Durham, 1949–67).

[43] Emden, *Cambridge*, p. 79; Le Neve, *Fasti*, VI, 113.

resort to arms. The duke of York was defeated and killed, as was his son Rutland, in the battle of Wakefield in Yorkshire on 30 December 1460. Soon after, York's eldest son, the eighteen-year-old Edward of March, sought a trial by battle with those who had defeated his father. A Lancastrian force was subdued by Edward at Mortimer's Cross on 2 or 3 February 1461. Edward's supporter, the earl of Warwick, suffered a reverse at the second battle of St Albans on 17 February, but Warwick was able to get away and join Edward in a race for London, where Edward was proclaimed King Edward IV by a few of his supporters gathered in Westminster Hall on 4 March. Edward soon set out after his Lancastrian opponents who were withdrawing to the north, and it was in Yorkshire, at Towton, on 29 March that Edward inflicted a major defeat upon the supporters of Lancaster. At the end of the day of fighting, Henry VI, his queen, Margaret, and their son, Prince Edward, were fleeing towards Scotland. This battle, fought in the archdiocese of William Booth, in effect made Edward IV king. It is permissible, though likely incorrect, to speculate that the Booths were feeling politically vulnerable in the spring of 1461 and in need of engaging in some inspired footwork. For the next few years King Edward and his great supporter, the earl of Warwick, would in part occupy themselves in stamping out resistance to Yorkist rule. The Booths, who had both served, for instance, as household chancellor to Margaret of Anjou, could hardly have failed to arouse some doubt about the depth of their loyalty to the new royal dynasty. There is, at the same time, no evidence that the Booths were unprepared to be reconciled with the new king. Not to be ignored are the actions of Lawrence Booth in raising local forces in June 1461 to drive back to their homeland a party of Scottish raiders who, under the leadership of Lords Dacre, Roos and Gray of Richemont, had penetrated as far into England as Brancepeth, which lay to the south of Durham.[44] William Booth, for his part, upon royal directive, ordered the clergy of the archdiocese of York to be ready to resist the invading Scots.[45]

---

[44] John Gillingham, *The Wars of the Roses* (Baton Rouge, Louisiana, 1981), p. 138.

[45] Reeves, *Lancastrian Englishmen*, p. 333.

In his efforts to minimize Lancastrian resistance in the northern parts of his kingdom, Edward IV had engaged in such gestures as making his way a few weeks after the battle of Towton to Durham, where he made Lawrence Booth his confessor in an attempt to secure the bishop's good will.[46] This overture of April was apparently successful to the extent that it contributed to Bishop Booth's participation with local levies in dispersing the Scottish and Lancastrian raiders who entered England from Scotland in June. At the end of the next month, Richard Neville, earl of Warwick, who almost certainly viewed Bishop Booth as being ill-disposed to Neville influence, was appointed warden of the East and West Marches toward Scotland.[47] Warwick had been King Edward's great supporter in the overthrow of the Lancastrian régime, and the earl's power was everywhere in the ascendant. As the balance of power in the north of England swung toward the Yorkists, in the late summer of 1461 King Edward made plans for an expedition to Wales which, in fact, was not carried out, as Edward left it to his lieutenants to represent his authority in Wales rather than leading the expedition in person. The king himself made preparations for the opening of the first parliament of his reign at Westminster on 4 November.

King Edward continued to be troubled by the support which the Scots were giving to the Lancastrian cause, and that support was being bolstered by King Louis XI of France, who was negotiating with Margaret of Anjou.[48] Margaret had gone to France in April 1462, but she was only able to take a modest armed force with her when she sailed to northern England in October. Edward was decidedly alarmed about an impending threat from Margaret in alliance with Scotland, and he raised defensive forces to resist any attack upon his kingdom from the north. Edward himself went to the north, arriving in York by the third week of November, and came a bit later to Durham where he became ill with

---

[46] A.E. Goodman, *The Wars of the Roses* (London, 1981), p. 57; C.D. Ross, *Edward IV* (Berkeley, 1974), pp. 45–6.

[47] R.L. Storey, 'Wardens of the Marches of England towards Scotland, 1377–1489', *English Historical Review*, 72 (1957), 614.

[48] P.J. Bradley, "Anglo-Scottish Relations during the Fifteenth Century, 1399–1485' (unpublished Emory University Ph.D. dissertation, 1983), pp. 229–38.

measles. Command of military activity fell to the earl of Warwick until the king recovered. The Lancastrian garrisons which in 1461 had been established in Dunstanburgh, Bamburgh, and Alnwick were unable to hold out against Edward's forces, and all were again under Yorkist control by January 1462. Generally events were progressing favourably for Edward. In February English ambassadors, including Bishop Booth, were appointed to meet with John MacDonald, earl of Ross, and other kinsmen of the young king of Scotland, James III.[49] The result of the ensuing negotiations is known as the treaty of Westminster-Ardtornish, sealed on 13 February and confirmed by Edward IV on 17 March, which called for Ross and others to assist Edward in the conquest of Scotland, the southern part of which would become a part of England.[50] Briefly stated, the scheme did not come to fruition. In the days after the sealing of the treaty, Bishop Booth was rewarded by Edward IV with a life-time share in the king's lordship of Wressle, Yorkshire, and the manor of Tooting Bec, Surrey, with the advowson of the church of Streatham in the same county.[51]

In the end, the Lancastrian threat to the north of England from Scotland, like the thoughts of an English conquest of Scotland, came to nothing, but Bishop Booth did not move through this period undisturbed, in spite of his apparent accommodation with Edward IV. On 7 December 1462, while in Durham, the king took the temporalities of the diocese of Durham into his own hands, and packed Bishop Booth off to Pembroke College, Cambridge, of which he was master and where he was now in effect under house arrest.[52]

---

[49] *C.P.R. (1461–67)*, p. 115; Thomas Rymer (ed.), *Foedera, conventiones, litterae et cujuscunque generis acta publica* . . . (17 vols, London, 1704–17), 11, 483–4.

[50] Bradley, 'Anglo-Scottish Relations', p. 230.

[51] *C.P.R. (1461–67)*, pp. 73, 113.

[52] Pollard, *North-Eastern England*, pp. 294–8; *35th DKR*, p. 112. Royal confiscation of episcopal temporalities was not a new form of putting political or fiscal pressure on bishops. Some venerable precedents from the reign of King Edward III would include the confiscation of the temporalities of Bishop John Grandisson of Exeter in 1349, those of Bishop Thomas de Lisle of Ely in 1356, and those of Bishop William Lynn of Chichester in 1365. John Aberth, *Criminal Churchmen in the Age of Edward III: The Case of Bishop Thomas de Lisle* (University Park, Pennsylvania, 1996), pp. 138–9, 183.

The temporalities of the diocese were placed under the administration of Sir John Fogge, Sir John Scott, respectively treasurer and controller of the king's household, and Thomas Colt, a chamberlain of the Exchequer.[53] Are we to suppose that Booth had been discovered acting in collusion with his former Lancastrian employers against the king? There is no evidence to bring us to such a conclusion. It seems far more likely that what was at work here was the Neville factor. The earl of Warwick still rankled over the dispute with Bishop Booth for possession of the lordship of Barnard Castle. Neville had lost the lordship to Booth in 1459, but had regained it in 1461 by royal grant despite the objections of Booth. The quarrel was sufficiently bitter that the earl from a position of strength and influence with the king at the end of 1462 was figuratively giving Bishop Booth's nose a mighty tweak. The king acquiesced in Neville assertiveness by acting in the bishop's place, through his possession of the temporalities of the see, to appoint as Justices of the Peace Richard Neville, earl of Warwick, Ralph Neville, earl of Westmorland, John Neville, Lord Montagu and others associated with the Neville family.[54] Lord Montagu was even made chief steward in the diocese. The king did at least leave Booth's chancellor, John Lounde, in office,[55] but Lounde had also been in the service of Bishop Robert Neville of Durham, of whose will he was one of the supervisors.

Booth remained in custody and without control of the temporalities of his diocese for more than fifteen months. Not until 15 April 1464 was he given his freedom, and two days afterwards he was authorized to enter and again occupy the temporalities of his bishopric.[56] King Edward apparently decided to effect a reconciliation with Bishop Booth because he was prepared to stand up against the wilfulness of the Neville earl of Warwick, as would be demonstrated

---

[53] *C.P.R. (1461–67)*, p. 215; *35th DKR*, p. 83.

[54] *35th DKR*, p. 89.

[55] *35th DKR*, p. 86. For Lounde (d. 1467), see A.B. Emden, *A Biographical Register of the University of Oxford to A.D. 1500* (3 vols, Oxford, 1957–9), 2, 1164–5.

[56] *C.P.R. (1461–67)*, pp. 325, 347, 374–5; *C.C.R. (1461–68)*, pp. 239, 242; *35th DKR*, pp. 78, 83, 86.

by Edward's secret marriage to Elizabeth Woodville on 1 May, while Warwick was negotiating for a French marriage for his king. Any suspicions of Booth as a Lancastrian collaborator are not reasonable in view of the restoration of Booth's temporalities in mid-April, because the Lancastrian threat was not quashed until the battle of Hedgeley Moor on 25 April, ten days after Booth's release, and the subsequent battle of Hexham on 15 May 1464. The tension with the Neville family was not yet, however, at an end, nor had the last been heard of the lordship of Barnard Castle.

On 12 September 1464 Archbishop William Booth of York died. The bishop who was translated to York as Booth's successor was none other than the brother of the earl of Warwick – George Neville, bishop of Exeter. It is difficult to imagine Bishop Booth of Durham welcoming such an event, coming in the aftermath of his half-brother's death. The trend of events in which Lawrence may have taken some comfort in the following years was the gradual diminution of Neville influence at the centre of power as King Edward found that he was able to distance himself from the earl of Warwick. The causes of a growing tension between the king and Warwick need not occupy us here, but it is important to acknowledge that development and to note that it ultimately evolved into an irreparable breach. So severe was the disaffection of Warwick by 1469, in fact, that he was preparing to overthrow King Edward.

In July 1469 Warwick, his brother, the archbishop of York, and the king's brother, George, duke of Clarence, cemented a conspiracy against the king with a marriage between Clarence and Isobel Neville, daughter and co-heiress of Warwick, performed by Archbishop Neville. A substantial force of rebels was raised, and the king, unable to coordinate resistance, found himself in the enforced tutelage of Warwick. With the king 'in commission', the kingdom simply could not be governed effectively by Warwick. King Edward gradually recovered his freedom of action, and by March 1470 was able to summon Warwick and Clarence to answer for their recent behaviour. Warwick and Clarence evaluated their chances of surviving the king's wrath, and fled to France and the protection of Louis XI. Edward was not fully able to consolidate his recovery of the kingdom but, on 6 June, Bishop Booth began another (brief) tenure in the lordship of Barnard Castle, thanks to a grant from

King Edward.[57] It was also at this time, on 18 July, that Lawrence Booth was first noted as being a councillor of Edward IV.[58]

Meanwhile, in France, King Louis brought Warwick and Clarence together with Queen Margaret to plan a Lancastrian recovery of England. Warwick, Clarence and other associates (but not Queen Margaret or her son Edward) embarked from La Hogue and landed in England at Dartmouth on 13 September 1470, while King Edward was in Yorkshire woefully unprepared for their arrival. With some difficulty, Edward escaped the kingdom accompanied by a clutch of supporters, including his youngest brother, Richard, duke of Gloucester. They made their way to Burgundian territory where they found refuge with Edward's and Richard's sister, Margaret, the wife of Duke Charles of Burgundy. In England, Henry VI was released from the Tower of London where he had been kept since his capture by Edward IV in 1465, and a 'readeption' government in the name of King Henry, but with Warwick wielding power, was set in place. As Warwick attempted to energize a government, Edward was laying plans with Burgundian aid for the operation that would enable him to regain his throne after losing it.

Edward landed on the Yorkshire coast on 14 March 1471. Soon after, Clarence defected from Warwick to the side of his royal brother. Edward moved southward, and on 11 April entered London where he secured the person of Henry VI. Three days later, on Easter Sunday at Barnet, Edward defeated Warwick in a battle that cost Warwick not only his tenuous hold on power but also his life. That very day, 14 April, Queen Margaret and Prince Edward, her son, landed in England. Edward IV caught up with Margaret and her army at Tewkesbury on 4 May and inflicted a crushing defeat upon the Lancastrians. Prince Edward was killed in the fighting, and Margaret was captured not long

---

[57] *35th DKR*, p. 97; A.J. Pollard, 'St Cuthbert and the Hog: Richard III and the County Palatine of Durham, 1471–85', in R.A. Griffiths and J. Sherborne (eds), *Kings and Nobles in the Later Middle Ages: A Tribute to Charles Ross* (Gloucester, 1986), p. 110.

[58] J.R. Lander, 'Council, Administration and Councillors, 1461 to 1485', *Bulletin of the Institute of Historical Research*, 32 (1959), 169.

after the battle. King Edward entered London in triumph on 21 May, and Henry VI died the same day in the Tower of London.[59] Booth had served as a councillor to Prince Edward when the prince was a child, and it is curious that just two months after Edward's violent death at Tewkesbury, Lawrence Booth was named among the administrators for the lands of the new Prince Edward of Wales, the son of Edward IV.[60] Within a few days, also in July 1471, Booth was named among several commissioners charged with treating for peace with Scotland and seeking to redress grievances of the citizenry of the Anglo-Scottish border.[61] Edward IV was pursuing the reestablishment of his government, and Booth was one of the ministers being employed in the process.

Bishop Booth had played no part in the 'readeption' government, and thus had no worry over royal reprisals. Nevertheless, the political reality was that King Edward had supporters to reward and the forfeited estates of the earl of Warwick were available for distribution. Among the lands for which a Neville claim might be asserted was the lordship of Barnard Castle, currently in the possession of Booth. The Dowager Countess Anne of Warwick might have a rival claim to put forward, as might the king's brothers, Clarence and Gloucester, who were anticipating being rewarded for assisting Edward in his recovery of the throne.[62] Countess Anne was not in a strong position to resist the king's will, but Clarence and Gloucester struggled vigorously for every available prize. It would seem that a link exists between the disposition of the lordship of Barnard Castle and Lawrence Booth's becoming chancellor of England. Booth became chancellor on 27 July 1473, and it was just about that time (although no documentary evidence survives to provide date or detail) that Gloucester entered into possession of Barnard Castle. There is a distinct possibility that Booth's elevation to the chancellorship was at least in part his reward for acquiescing in Gloucester's adding Barnard Castle to his complex of northern estates. The great seal was

---

[59] For these events, see P.W. Hammond, *The Battles of Barnet and Tewkesbury* (Gloucester, 1990).

[60] *C.P.R. (1467–77)*, p. 283.

[61] Joseph Bain (ed.), *Calendar of Documents relating to Scotland* (4 vols, Edinburgh, 1881–8), 4, 282–3.

[62] Pollard, 'St Cuthbert and the Hog', in *Kings and Nobles*, pp. 110–11.

delivered by the king's hands to his new chancellor, Booth, on 27 July in the refectory of the house of the Franciscan friars at Stamford, Lincolnshire.[63]

It has been argued that Bishop Booth of Durham, as chancellor, and the lord of Barnard Castle, Richard of Gloucester, had a cool relationship, largely because Booth was not pleased to have parted with Barnard Castle and because he was involved in seeking peace with Scotland, while Duke Richard had become lord of Barnard Castle and viewed Scotland with aggressive hostility.[64] It has also been argued, quite to the contrary, that Bishop Booth worked comfortably with the duke of Gloucester and was even partial towards Duke Richard's territorial ambitions. The latter view is bolstered by the evidence that Booth supported Gloucester in the coercion of Elizabeth Howard, widow of John de Vere, earl of Oxford (executed for treason in 1462), into surrendering her legitimately held property to the duke.[65] A way to find consistency in Bishop Booth's actions is to postulate that his position was that of a steadfast servant of his king. If Edward wished to seek a harmonious coexistence with Scotland, Booth would work to that end; and if Edward made no effort to temper his younger brother's acquisitiveness, Booth would offer no ethical objections. Booth was being the quintessentially supportive and obedient administrative extension of his royal master. Such a temperament of dedication would also assist in comprehending Booth's steady enjoyment of Edward IV's patronage.

To be chancellor of England was indeed to be recognized and rewarded, for it made Bishop Booth the most lofty governmental servant of the king. In December 1473 Booth gained a share in the patronage concerning the next vacant prebend at St George's Chapel, Windsor, and in March 1474 he was granted a share in the right to collate a cleric to the next vacant prebend in St Stephen's Chapel, Westminster.[66] On St Cuthbert's Day, 1474, a day always

[63] *C.C.R. (1468–76)*, pp. 319–20.

[64] Pollard, 'St Cuthbert and the Hog', in *Kings and Nobles*, p. 115.

[65] M.A. Hicks, 'The Last Days of Elizabeth, Countess of Oxford', *English Historical Review*, 103 (1988), 76–95.

[66] *C.P.R. (1467–77)*, pp. 411, 437, 439.

special in the diocese of Durham, Booth was rewarded by the king for good service with permission to build stone walls and towers around the episcopal mansion of Bridgecourt in Battersea parish, Surrey.[67]

Booth served as chancellor until 27 May 1474, but the brevity of Booth's term in itself necessarily suggests nothing qualitative about his performance, and there appears to be no evidence to support Lord Campbell's assertion in the nineteenth century that Booth was dismissed from the chancellorship for incompetence.[68] Lord Campbell was misled by a Chancery joke recorded in the continuations of the Crowland Abbey chronicle about several chancellors which mentioned that Booth became weary of the work, and the joke was that the chancellors did not in fact do the hard work, but rather it was the Master of the Rolls who carried the burden.[69] If Booth was regarded as incompetent by Edward IV he likely would not have been closely engaged for some three years in the Anglo-Scottish negotiations that culminated in the treaty of Edinburgh of 26 October 1474.[70] In fact, just two months after leaving the chancellorship, Booth was appointed to a highly important diplomatic commission to deal with the ambassadors of King James III of Scotland over the Scottish ship *Le Salvator*, which had been wrecked off Bamburgh in a storm and then plundered and the passengers held for ransom.[71] The commissioners were also to negotiate for a marriage (ultimately unaccomplished) between the son and heir of King James, also called James, and Edward IV's daughter, Cecily. These assigned tasks were stages leading to the treaty of Edinburgh. Nor, we should think, if Booth were considered to be incompetent by his king would he have been appointed to serve on the Council that ruled England

---

[67] *Calendar of Charter Rolls (1427–1516)*, p. 242.

[68] John, Lord Campbell, *The Lives of the Lord Chancellors and Keepers of the Great Seal of England* (8 vols, London, 1846–69), 1, 392.

[69] Nicholas Pronay and John Cox (eds), *The Crowland Chronicle Continuations: 1459–1486* (London, 1986), pp. 84, 132–3.

[70] Pollard, *North-Eastern England*, p. 231; Bradley, 'Anglo-Scottish Relations', pp. 253–65; Norman Macdougall, *James III* (Edinburgh, 1982), pp. 116–17.

[71] Bain (ed.), *Documents Relating to Scotland*, 4, 287–9, 304.

while Edward IV was on military campaign in France in the summer of 1475.[72] Every step forward in Booth's career, moreover, is evidence of administrative ability.

There is a clear irony in the final triumph in Booth's career. He had been made bishop of Durham by the Lancastrian government as something of a counterweight to the previous bishop, Robert Neville, and his powerful family. On 8 June 1476 George Neville, archbishop of York and brother of the slain 'Kingmaker', died, and the Yorkist government of Edward IV secured the appointment of Lawrence Booth as the new archbishop.[73] Two rival royal dynasties had now used Booth in an effort to diminish the influence of the Neville family. Booth was translated from Durham to York on 31 July, granted the temporalities of the see on 8 October, and formally enthroned on 4 September 1477. Lawrence thus came in his turn to fill the place vacated by the death in 1464 of his half-brother William. Lawrence was the first bishop of Durham to be translated to York. One of Booth's first activities in 1476 as the new archbishop was to assist with the removal of the bodies of the king's father and brother, killed at Wakefield in 1460, from their graves at Pontefract Priory to the family burial place at Fotheringhay Castle.[74]

The archdiocese of York was substantially larger than the diocese of Durham, and was subdivided into five archdeaconries rather than two, as in the diocese of Durham. The cathedral church of the archbishop of York was served by a secular chapter of clergy, while the cathedral of Durham was served by a chapter made up of Benedictine monks. The four major dignitaries of the cathedral chapter at York were the dean, who will be discussed presently, the precentor, the chancellor and the treasurer. The precentor, whose main area of responsibility was the music and song of York Minster, was William Eure, who had been appointed by Archbishop William Booth and who served throughout the tenure of Archbishop

---

[72] Pollard, *North-Eastern England*, p. 61.

[73] Le Neve, *Fasti*, VI, 5.

[74] C.D. Ross, *Edward IV* (Berkeley, 1974), p. 271; C.L. Scofield, *The Life and Reign of Edward the Fourth* (2 vols, London, 1923), 2, 167.

Lawrence.[75] Lawrence Booth did not appoint a chancellor while he was archbishop, because Dr Thomas Chaundeler, a theologian, was in office when Booth became archbishop, and was still in office after Booth's death.[76] The treasurer of the cathedral, who was charged to maintain and keep safe the treasures of the cathedral used in services, such as altar cloths, vestments, plate, relics and the bread and wine, was John Pakenham, whose appointment had been made by Archbishop William Booth, but in 1477 Archbishop Lawrence placed in office Thomas Portington,[77] who would later be named an executor of Booth's will.

As archbishop of York, Booth did not drop out of royal service. In a routine matter, for instance, he was directed in 1479 to appoint collectors of the tax voted by the clergy of the northern convocation to serve the king's needs.[78] He had been ordered to do the same thing in 1475 as bishop of Durham.[79] Booth continued to receive royal appointments to commissions of the peace, just as he had when bishop of Durham.[80] Booth was a witness when Edward IV created his nephew, Edward, the first-born son of his brother Richard, duke of Gloucester, to be earl of Salisbury on 15 February 1478.[81] A more sensitive situation in which Booth served Edward IV arose from his order on 27 October 1479 to the official of his consistory court, Dr William Poteman, to prohibit any worship or display of veneration in York Minster at the place where the statue of King Edward's royal predecessor, Henry VI, had stood.[82]

---

[75] Le Neve, *Fasti*, VI, 11.

[76] *Ibid.*, VI, 9.

[77] *Ibid.*, VI, 14.

[78] *Calendar of Fine Rolls (1471–85)*, pp. 189–94.

[79] *Ibid.*, pp. 115–18.

[80] *C.P.R. (1452–61)*, pp. 662, 673, 682–4; *ibid.* (1461–67), p. 576; *ibid.* (1467–77), pp. 632, 637–38; *ibid.* (1476–85), pp. 574, 579–80. It may be noted that when appointed a Justice of the Peace in Yorkshire between 1477 and 1479, Booth was on commissions to which Richard, duke of Gloucester was also appointed.

[81] *C.P.R. (1476–85)*, pp. 67–8.

[82] G.W. Kitchin (ed.), *The Records of the Northern Convocation* (Durham, 1907), pp. 349–50. For William Poteman, see Emden, *Oxford*, 3, 1506–7.

Owing to the survival of the register of Lawrence Booth's official acts as archbishop, it is readily possible to offer examples of his using patronage to be a mentor to members of his family. William Worsley, a Booth kinsman who studied civil law at Cambridge and who was, fittingly, a canon and ultimately dean of St Paul's and was buried in St Paul's Cathedral, London, after his death in 1499, became archdeacon of Nottingham in the archdiocese of York just two months after Lawrence Booth became archbishop.[83] Dr Robert Booth (died 1488) has been mentioned as a canon of York and prebendary of Wetwang,[84] but Lawrence had earlier made him a canon and prebendary of Ampleforth (January 1477), which he gave up for the Wetwang benefice (February 1478).[85] Robert had already also held two successive canonries at Beverley, thanks to the patronage of Lawrence, when in July 1477 he was elected to the deanship of the cathedral chapter at York.[86] Robert so enjoyed the confidence of Archbishop Booth that he would be named an executor of Booth's will when the document came to be drawn up on 28 September 1479.[87] When Robert gave up the prebend of Ampleforth, it was bestowed upon Thomas Booth (died 1501), a Cambridge bachelor of canon law whom Lawrence had already provided to the rectory of Carlton in Lindrick, Nottinghamshire.[88] Ralph Booth, mentioned above as archdeacon of Durham, became in addition in 1478 the archdeacon of York (or of the West Riding) by the act of Lawrence.[89] Three clerks of the Clifton family obtained canonries early in Lawrence's archiepiscopate: Gervase (1 May 1478) and William (3 July 1479) becoming canons of Southwell, and Robert (2 November 1479) a canon

[83] Borthwick Institute of Historical Research, York Register 22, f. 241; Emden, *Cambridge*, p. 651.

[84] See above n. 28.

[85] York Register 22, ff. 242, 244v.

[86] *Ibid.*, ff. 251–251v; Le Neve, *Fasti*, VI, 8.

[87] James Raine (ed.), *The Historians of the Church of York and its Archbishops* (3 vols, London, Rolls Series, 1879–94), 3, 335.

[88] York Register 22, ff. 245, 270v; Emden, *Cambridge*, p. 80; Le Neve, *Fasti*, VI, 29.

[89] York Register 22, ff. 244v, 246; Le Neve, *Fasti*, VI, 19.

of York.[90] These were not the only men, to be sure, whom Lawrence patronized as archbishop, but the kinsmen are too numerous to be unobtrusive. Nothing suggests that Lawrence did not seek out worthy men to appoint to benefices, but today's negative notions of nepotism were no bar to advancement if Booth kinship was accompanied by worthiness.

The story of Lawrence Booth exemplifies clearly the career paradigm both of a highly successful ecclesiastic and of his family over several thriving generations: the study of law, common, civil or canon; the development and exercise of administrative skills; the struggle up the ladder of ecclesiastical preferment; and the mentoring hand extended to kinsmen seeking to realize their potential in the career race. On the basis of his many accomplishments, it could be argued that Lawrence was the family star. If he was conscious on Friday morning, St Dunstan's Day (19 May), 1480, as he lay dying at Southwell,[91] he would have been justified in feeling a sense of satisfaction over his earthly career, for he had been household chancellor to a queen, councillor to kings and heirs to the throne, keeper of the privy seal, chancellor of England, a diplomat, a bishop and an archbishop, and the survivor of mighty political storms that had buffeted the kingdom. He could also have taken familial comfort in knowing that his mortal remains would shortly be laid to rest beside those of his half-brother, William, in the thirteenth-century Vavasour chantry chapel dedicated to St John the Baptist and located toward the west end of the south aisle within the nave of Southwell Minster, which William had further endowed and perhaps had enlarged or rebuilt. That William had provided for construction work is uncertain, but he had provided endowment for his obit and a Jesus Mass, which was apparently celebrated at an altar adjacent to his tomb. Lawrence provided for the addition of a chantry foundation and altar to the chapel, dedicated to the Virgin and St Cuthbert, so that priests would celebrate daily the divine services beneficial to his soul and the souls of others, including

---

[90] York Register 22, ff. 247v, 249v–250.

[91] It is recorded that he died between 11.00 a.m. and noon. Raine (ed.), *Historians of the Church of York*, 2, 439.

his parents and the king and queen.[92] Lawrence also provided either for the further enlargement of the chapel in which William was buried or for the building of a chapel to enclose the tombs of William and himself, which came to be known as the Booth Chapel. Today the chapel and the chantry altars are gone, as are the tombs of the Archbishops Booth of York. Such utter absence from view is a powerful contrast to the visibility and striking accomplishments of Lawrence Booth during his energetic life.

---

[92] *C.P.R. (1476–85)*, p. 255; G.H. Cook, *Mediaeval Chantries and Chantry Chapels* (London, 1963), p. 196; A.H. Thompson, 'The Certificates of the Chantry Commissioners for the College of Southwell in 1546 and 1548, with an Introduction and Notes', *Transactions of the Thoroton Society*, 15 (1911), 87–92.

5

RICHARD III, RICHARD NIXON AND THE BRUTALITY OF FIFTEENTH-CENTURY POLITICS: A DISCUSSION*

Colin Richmond

I thought I would start with a brief test about contemporary American literature. From which contemporary and fairly local American writer does the following exchange come:

'So you've been jealous', said Laura Wong.
'The opposite', replied Clara. 'The people I've been intimate with to him are like the folks in the history books. And suppose Richard III had gotten into *your* wife's pants when she was a girl?'

This is one of the more bizarre Richard III references encountered, and I thought you would enjoy it. So which writer is this? He is not too distant from here – Chicagoan; it is Saul Bellow, in a story called 'A Theft' included in a recent collection, *Something to Remember Me By*. It is a rather serious collection of older stories that have previously been published separately. But this is a new story, and it is a good line to remember, 'And suppose Richard III had gotten into *your* wife's pants when she was a girl'. I am not quite sure what it means, except that he is trying to emphasize that *Richard III*, that is, Shakespeare, is using

---

* This is based on a taped recording of Colin Richmond's talk and the ensuing discussion, with minor amendments designed to make them more fully intelligible to those who were not present. Those who took part included Laura Blanchard, Ralph A. Griffiths, DeLloyd J. Guth, Craig Levin, Sharon Michalove, Mary Miller, Philip Morgan, A. Compton Reeves and Colin Richmond.

Richard III as a historical figure, which is not as I want us to think of him. That consigns him – does it not? – to the past in the way that Clara is here thinking of her earlier lovers. She is on her fourth husband in the story.

This is a complicated paper because it is mainly written on these little guest-room slips, and it follows the William Burroughs method of lecturing: that is, the slips of paper are selected in a fairly random way. I had thought that I might substitute 'morality' for 'brutality' in the title of this piece – 'Richard III and the *Morality* of Fifteenth-Century Politics'. I have been moving in that direction over the past fortnight, but I think that DeLloyd Guth's paper (see chapter 3) rather moved me back again. That should become clear in the sequel.

There are about four layers to this paper, all of them incompatible: 1. Last night's sleepless thoughts; 2. DeLloyd Guth's exciting paper juxtaposing the civil with war or perhaps, in the terminology that I have used for the title, brutality; 3. The idea that has come to me in the last fortnight of examining, or trying to think about, the civil servants or the councillors who were active or present in those months of April and May 1483: what were they thinking? What were they doing, particularly in relation to the brutality, if that is the right word, the usurpation, or the means of Richard's taking the crown; 4. The original idea which I began with, concerning the nature and origins of what I think is detectable, that is, perhaps some increasing or enhanced brutality of the politics of fifteenth-century England.

Now, I know you would not like it, and I am not asking you to think of Richard III as Richard Nixon, though you are perfectly entitled to do so. But, I do want us to ponder the idea of the connection between the usurpation of Richard III – especially, perhaps, the murder of the princes – and the battle of Bosworth, or, more specifically, Richard's defeat at the battle of Bosworth. Just as I want you, as it were, to ponder the connection between the Watergate burglary and the impeachment of the president. Consider these with three possibilities in mind. Firstly, is the connection uncertain? Is it a close-run thing between the usurpation of Richard III and his defeat at Bosworth and, alternatively, between the Watergate break-in and the president's impeachment? Secondly, might it be inevitable that one follows the other, and, thirdly, is it morally necessary that one should follow the other? The only thing missing from Richard III's story is a rape. How much we would like that!

I think this is something well worth thinking about, because I want to believe in the moral connection between Richard's defeat at Bosworth and the nature of his usurpation. I want to say that the nature of the usurpation brings defeat with it, because in certain ways that were sufficiently immoral according to fifteenth-century lights, or unconventional within political mores, that is why he was stranded at Bosworth. I would like to believe that. Whether it is true or not is something we have to wonder about.

I said you must not think about Nixon in terms of Richard III, but there are important parallels here, because Richard Nixon was a man who achieved a lot, did he not? He ended the war in Vietnam, did he not? He opened up relations with China. He did a number of things which I am sure made him an active, 'good' president. Many people wish to say that Richard III was a good king. And I would not argue with them – or that he had the potential for good, or rather for achievements, of which there were some. I worry a lot about the way historians talk about such themes, for example, about King John and the manner in which the last generation of historians have said that 'he was a good administrator', as if that somehow is sufficient.

'Richard III isn't Henry V': I am not quite sure what the significance of that is. I think it has something to do with Henry V as the model king of the fifteenth century. In what ways might one want to think about the differences in kingship between the two?

Part 2 is about brutality and fifteenth-century politics, the original idea I had for this paper. I want to explore this a little, because if Richard is brutal in the way that he acquires the throne, what precedent is there for good behaviour similar to that found earlier in the fifteenth century? I do not want to go back further than the fifteenth century. There is a lot of good writing: John Gillingham has written a splendid piece on chivalry, and on the difference, perhaps, that the idea of chivalry brought to political behaviour in the twelfth and thirteenth centuries. What John says is similar to Maitland's idea that the later Middle Ages were an age of blood, rather than the early Middle Ages, which were more civilized. There are longer-term views to be taken on this question of how you behave politically, but I just want you to think about political behaviour in the Wars of the Roses.

When does brutalism enter into political life, if it does? It is not clear in the case of Henry VI: we do not think of him as a brutal king, do we? But there is the evidence of those hangings in 1447, when Gloucester's people were strung up and then cut down? What about Tiptoft? He ordered the beheading of the earl of Desmond in 1468 as well as the far more notorious impalements of 1470. Tiptoft's sort of behaviour is often seen as un-English, Italianate.

Then there is Edward IV and the breaking of the sanctuary of Tewkesbury Abbey in May 1471, taking out those diehard Lancastrians who had taken refuge there. Charles Ross says not too much should be made of this incident as a lapse from Edward's record of clemency to his opponents. The victims were all men who had shown themselves to be irreconcilable and nearly all had been pardoned by Edward in the past, only to abuse his generosity. Given their records, they could have expected little else and by contemporary standards deserved little else. It may be the first time sanctuary is broken in the Wars of the Roses. This invasion of sacred space continues, notoriously on Monday, 16 June 1483 at Westminster; and although it does not happen, the threat is there. But Henry VII is bad at this, the invasion of sacred space. Of course, sacred time is being invaded as well: that is what the Reformation is all about and this is a much more important issue than Charles Ross allowed.

Now a murder that Charles Ross did not mention in his *Edward IV*, and Ralph Griffiths only just mentioned in his *The Reign of King Henry VI* (London, 1981), must be examined. It is the beheading of Osbert Mountford (or Mundford) at Rysbank on 25 June 1460. Ralph Griffiths says (p. 859) that Osbert Mountford was captured in a Yorkist raid on Sandwich, and 'was conveyed to Rysbank tower and beheaded'. At least Miss Scofield said, many years before (*The Life and Reign of Edward the Fourth* [2 vols, London, 1923], I, 76), 'This deed seemed a little out of keeping with the desire to avoid bloodshed which Coppini [the papal legate] claimed for the Yorkists' (he was going to come across with the Yorkists the following day, 26 June, I think when they set out to invade England). That was a cold-blooded murder. Mountford had been captured in Sir John Dynham's descent on Sandwich a few weeks earlier, at the beginning of June, and Osbert Mountford had been assembling a force to oppose Warwick, who was in control at Calais. That had been prevented by Dynham's expedition and Mountford had been captured two or three weeks before. So it was not a hot-blooded killing, because of the interval between

Mountford's capture and his beheading before the Yorkist invasion. I cannot see any legal or other reason for that killing, and I came to it, as I come to almost everything, through the Pastons; that is, the only surviving expense account of John Paston I is for the accounting year 1457/8 and I have used it very heavily in my second volume on the Pastons (*The Paston Family in the Fifteenth Century: Fastolf's Will* [Cambridge, 1996], p. 27). One of his expenses was 2s 1d expended at Thetford in meeting with Osbert Mountford. They knew each other fairly well and, again, this is where one would love to have had a tape recorder to listen to what they were discussing at that point. There is rather more to this than perhaps meets the eye. I do not want to dwell too long on the possibility of local politics entering into a decision to execute, or rather murder, Osbert Mountford. However, there were local disputes in which the earl of Warwick was himself involved, not in the late fifties but in the early sixties, and of course he was involved earlier and it may be that this vindictiveness – the word, I think, could be applied to that killing at Rysbank – might result not so much from national politics, as we like to call them, but from local. There is more to it than that even, because one of the interesting things is that Osbert Mountford's brother-in-law was Andrew Trollope. He was noted for piracy, among many other activities, and as the man who deserted Warwick at Ludford in October 1459. I think this because there seem to be other killings at Calais in 1459/60, that is, between the disaster at Ludford in October 1459 and the killing of Mountford in June 1460. In that interval, some unpleasant things were done to people in the Calais Pale under Warwick's command.

This of course would fit very nicely with Ralph Griffiths's first paper (see chapter 1) about looking at the periphery, the dominions – maybe these brutalities had first been encountered in the dominions, not in the central part of the polity. I do not think the chroniclers make any comment one way or the other. Even if Calais records, for example, existed more completely than they do, I doubt whether they would reveal anything about this. I have raised these cases because, leaving aside the earl of Worcester, and indeed Edward IV at Tewkesbury, I have not mentioned the killings or the murders or the executions after Edgecote by Warwick, which are straightforwardly brutal because they do not have legal grounds; but in this case I am looking back a little further to consider the earl of Warwick earlier. What is the connection – if there is a connection – between the earl of Warwick's behaviour and perhaps that of Richard?

Let me come to the third topic, in which I became interested a couple of weeks ago, about councillors and which, I think, does neatly overlap with DeLloyd Guth's discussion of what is 'civil'. I am thinking about 'civil' and a 'civil service', so to speak, and the words that he has used about it: continuity, professionalism, security, predictability, and the men who are of that tradition. Considering these men in 1483, in April, May and June, they were the people who wanted to maintain the *civil* situation in the face of the brutalities, as it were, the upsets, the discontinuities, the insecurities, the unpredictabilities and such like. There are some fascinating connections to be made here. It may be significant, may it not, that Reynold Bray moves into the shadows (was that the phrase?)? Was Richard III too much for this epitome of all these civil virtues and qualities? If 1485 is the victory of the civil servants, which I believe it to be, they are Yorkist civil servants because, as I have argued many times before, Henry VII – however Welsh he was, however much from the periphery – is a *Yorkist* king, because he is surrounded by a network of Yorkist civil servants. So, it is the behaviour of these people that I have put under a little scrutiny in the last few weeks. Unfortunately, there are no conclusions to be reached. As you might expect, there would have been a variety of responses from these people to what they were witnessing in April, May and June of 1483. Some of them were participants as well as witnesses. We could consider Sir Roger Townshend (see Charles Moreton's 'The Diary of a Late Fifteenth-century Lawyer', chapter 2), who petitioned for the retention of the post of king's sergeant-at-law the day after the coronation. He was someone who clearly settled for things. He was not a civil servant in the proper sense, but, nevertheless, I think he would embody the values that DeLloyd Guth refers to. What about his companion, Sir Thomas Bryan, who, I think, was a councillor and Townshend's circuit companion from 1488? Bryan was, in 1483, a councillor of Edward IV and then, I think, of Richard III. So he was another of these people who might settle for things. The question I would like to ask is, at what price, in terms of morality, did they settle? I am thinking here, of course, about Watergate; there are John Deans and there are Gordon Liddys. There is no reason to suppose that there were not such persons in the spring of 1483. It is rather difficult to locate any secure information about who may have been active in and on the Council in April 1483, before Richard of Gloucester came to London.

Those days in 1483 were obviously terribly important. We know from the commissions that were issued to collect a subsidy who were active. Rosemary Horrox has put these people under some scrutiny; but there were people the commission in the southern counties and the northern counties had excluded so we cannot discuss them. It is likely that – and Charles Ross has said this, looking at Edward IV's funeral and who was present there, and using J.R. Lander's article from 1959 ('Council, Administration and Councillors, 1461–1485', *Bull. Institute of Historical Research*, XXXII, 138–80) about the councillors of Edward IV, Richard III and Henry VII which I have used here – there could have been a lot of councillors in London in April. What I want you to think about is not just a handful of Woodvilles and William, Lord Hastings and a few officers of the Crown, but the others who were councillors at the death of Edward IV, and about what happened to them. As Charles Ross says, there was likely to have been a substantial body of such councillors. I could use all sorts of people, some of whom have surfaced in our couple of days here. John Wood (see chapter 6), for example; and Sir John Elrington surfaced in a case that Charles Moreton refers to, or rather Elrington's widow surfaced, but that may well be because he was caught up in that epidemic at the end of 1483. He would be a good test case, keeper of the Wardrobe, treasurer of the Household, about fifty years old in 1483; he lost those offices in the course of the spring of 1483, and yet he was made knight of the body by Richard and was dead by 12 December 1483, so it is hard to know a great deal about him. There are others, and this is where bishops come in. Who are the Lawrence Booths of 1483? Who were the William Worsleys – he is a favourite character of mine, and Compton Reeves mentions him as one of those relatives of the Booths who was promoted and became dean of St Paul's. He is a favourite character of mine because there is a portrait of him in a very obscure place in the Museum of London – remnant of a wall-painting from his house at Hackney with him kneeling, a very unusual survival since the house was bombed in the Second World War. But he got caught up in the Perkin Warbeck affair in 1495. He was, as it were, one of those men who somehow got involved in the brutalities rather than kept to the civil route. One example of these councillor-bishops is William Dudley, who was bishop of Durham in 1483. He had been dean of the Chapel Royal at St George's, and indeed sang the Mass of the Virgin at Edward IV's funeral in St George's

Chapel. He was a committed Yorkist in 1471, because he brought troops out at Doncaster on Edward's return to England in March 1471. He was the younger son of John Sutton, Lord Dudley, who was still going strong as a councillor in his eighties in the spring of 1483, an Oxford man, and bishop of Durham since 1476. He was made chancellor of Oxford on 20 October 1483; he died on 29 November 1483. You cannot quite tell, but it looks as if he was making an accommodation with the brutal Richard.

The best example, of course, and I think it is the critical one, is John Russell, bishop of Lincoln, and chancellor under Richard III. He was a Wykehamist, bachelor of canon and civil law, first chancellor of Oxford University for life, appointed immediately after the death of William Dudley – that is characteristic of sycophantic Oxford University but a good indication of who they think is really in league with Richard. He was a great builder at Oxford: if you go to the Divinity Schools or you come to the nave of St Mary's then you are looking, really, at work that Russell brought to completion. He was about fifty-five in 1483, and was a man who, Thomas More said, was the 'best learned man of his time, a wise man and a good and of much experience'. I think one might get further with him if you read all the books that he possessed. We know of sixteen or seventeen books that he owned. Here is almost the epitome, I think, of a *civil servant* – not quite as much an epitome as Bray, perhaps, but, nevertheless, he embodied almost all that was best, examined from one angle, in fifteenth-century life. What did this mean?

I hoped to learn more from looking at these councillors. I do not think one can get a very long way, but I think one can get much further than I have got, at least by thinking along these sorts of lines. I am disappointed because Richard III is emerging in a more favourable light than I had thought of him over the last thirty years. If people like Russell were willing to tolerate the brutalities of 1483. . . ? I quote a letter from Bill Spears of Claystowe, West Sussex. He must have written to me ten or twelve years ago about Richard III and said, 'after some years at a ringside seat at various coups in the Middle East, I find nothing particularly incomprehensible about the events of June 1483'. I would hate to agree with that, but being a very fair-minded sort of fellow I bring it to you to think about.

So I end with these sorts of questions, trying to connect the two things that I began with, namely, the usurpation and Bosworth, or the burglary and the impeachment. Which is the more comprehensible or, *vice versa*, the less comprehensible: the Watergate burglary or the impeachment? Those Americans among you, what did you find most incomprehensible in American political life? – because I think the same question can be asked about the usurpation and the defeat of Richard at Bosworth. Which is more comprehensible to us, as it were? By usurpation I think I must also add 'murder of the princes' as a part of that process, and my final note that says, 'O for a Ricardian Woodward and Bernstein'.

DISCUSSION

Q There never was an impeachment.

Richmond Oh, right. That shows how ignorant I am. He went before that, didn't he? It was a threat, was it?

Guth I would challenge that. Technically, there was impeachment, because impeachment means accusation. There was a formal accusation lodged in the House of Representatives. It seems to me that, from a formalistic and legalistic vantage point, that constitutes impeachment. It did not, of course, constitute trial and conviction.

Richmond I hope I haven't opened up wounds here . . .

Griffiths The great difference, though, is that the Nixon episode was played out in front of the public, with television and so on, whereas in 1483 it is very difficult to know at what stage even the very well-informed people in London and Westminster began to realize what was going on. The Crowland Chronicler talks about people scurrying up and down corridors, poking their heads into doors they should not, reporting the mechanism of rumour, if you like, and – Charles Ross made this very important point – how can we expect to understand fully what happened, because necessarily it was all behind-closed-doors stuff. On the Nixon case . . .

Richmond No, not the original . . .

Griffiths Not the original, but after a certain point the drama is open, it's public, isn't it.

Blanchard But it took many agonizing years for it to become open to the public. My sense of those times was a long time of saying 'enough, just confess, let us get on with our lives'.

Griffiths But people wouldn't have been in that state of knowledge in 1483 until well afterward.

Guth There is some argument that Russell may have been the author of the Crowland Chronicle . . .

Richmond Well, it was Margaret Condon's case, as I recall it.

Levin Mountford was one of the Calais bandits. It wouldn't have been hard for Warwick to have found a quick set of witnesses to say, 'yes, he robbed us in broad daylight', a sort of a drumhead trial.

Richmond Yes, that may yet be close to what happened, but then Warwick has been pirating right, left and centre in '57/8.

Griffiths We haven't raised this question: if brutality is a mode of behaviour, and increasing brutality, as indicated, how does one explain such action? Charles Ross was making an allied point. He was trying to be very fair and saying that Richard III's behaviour was part of a pattern which had established itself, he felt (wrongly, I believe), at the very beginning of the fifteenth century, even in the late fourteenth century, whereas you've made some really good points, haven't you, which would indicate that brutality is something that can seep into itself: it seeps in from the beginning of the Yorkist period. Maybe Warwick himself had a lot to answer for; he was very much Edward's mentor in a crucial stage in his career, and some of the incidents from 1459–69 come back to Warwick all the time. I don't know whether brutality is acquired in that way. We don't know today, do we, whether Richard picked this up similarly. I have a feeling that it's a Yorkist failing – in the 1450s; it's especially common in this aristocratic circle that remains aristocratic even when the Yorkists become kings.

Richmond And I think one might turn it round, don't you, in the sense that one should admire, actually, perhaps, the restraint and adhesion to conventions or norms in politics through the '50s, anyway, because even the St Albans attainder and so on goes for the least damage. It isn't until perhaps '59–'60 . . . and maybe that desertion, that peculiar happening at Ludford, that breaks some restraint. I think you're right, but McFarlane would always have said, look at the other side of it and see how well-behaved, perhaps, English politicians are. I think John

Watts, from an entirely different angle, would endorse that sort of a view, a much younger man writing. I think he would rather endorse that, the way that politicians tried to hold things together for a very long period, namely right until '59–'60. But Ludford might be a critical moment here.

Guth Running through all of this is something that is fascinating, ethereal . . . the emergence of new norms; that is to say, during the Watergate period we saw mass culture participating in a shift of norms, a sense of right and wrong. The seeming complexity of the legal definition, which will be strict and which will come back to the little argument we just had, on the one hand, but there is the broader issue of normativity as a source of law, that is to say, the area of tolerance for activity that a society allows. The parameters are drawn, and these parameters are moved in and out, and many people were pushing them out at the time of Watergate, saying 'why they're all that way, everybody is like that'; so you push the parameters out. And then in a sense the legal process, once it got under way, pushed those parameters back, and people said, 'well, even if they do all behave that way, they ought to be accountable'. So there is that kind of movement in all cultures in all times and places and I think concerning brutality, which we're talking about here. Is it learned or schooled behaviour? In that case you'd expect a war veteran coming back to Henry V's reign to be very schooled in violence; I mean, God, the carnage, and the mud and the mess of that French campaign. And so, I guess, the statisticians among us, the quantifiers could say, 'let's see if crime increases, violence increases, in civil culture afterwards'. There are these people who came back from Vietnam; did *they* have a predilection, did they have to work it out of their systems or whatever, and have nightmares? So we're dealing with, then, to pick up on Ralph Griffiths's point, if this were 1460, 1459, people who would begin to reschool themselves again to move the parameters out, to tolerate more violence, to tolerate more brutality. We're not talking about law, now, strictly speaking – martial law, canon law, customary law, or certainly common law – but that area of normativity. If they aren't pushing it out now, before it reaches the legal limits, and then the law begins to pull it back in. I think they're pushing it out from 1460 onward. I think we have to look for the events, the participation; are there opportunities that pre-date this emergence of greater brutality, are there events that would allow people to become more violent, to become more tolerant of brutality? The other way is to say, well, it's in all of us, original sin; given the opportunity and the necessity we'll 'stick it to them'.

Richmond This brings us straight back to the disappearance of the princes. This must remain a critical piece of evidence, as rumour, for this question of expanding/contracting parameters.

Guth We're all watching it every day, it's on television, we're reading about it. But 1483 was not a 'popular' (that is, of the people) event?

Richmond We're not interested in them here.

Guth We have to be if we're assessing rumour and how effective rumour is, and how this will affect allegiance, and wondering how this king is going to be my liege lord or not.

Richmond But I think we're looking at the political nature here. If we're thinking that Richard losing at Bosworth is somehow connected to his earlier behaviour: this is a very contentious area but the possibility of people not turning out for the crowned and anointed king, that's an unusual sort of thing, so, if we're looking at that I think we should say 'is that connected with his behaviour in some way prior to Bosworth?' Hitherto, I've always argued that the murder of William, Lord Hastings and the presumed murder of the princes do break boundaries of conventional political behaviour, however much we might wish to say 'let's look at new brutalities' from 1459: that is, what Richard gets up to, certainly on 13 June 1483. William, Lord Hastings knew his English politics inside-out, backwards and forwards. We can't ever think of him as someone likely to be taken by surprise, because he's been at the forefront of everything since 1459. I think the image that's been cultivated by Shakespeare and others – William, Lord Hastings's image is one of a man who screws Jane Shore and enjoys himself – is not the case: he is a very experienced, very in-depth politician. He must know everything. And yet he's taken completely by surprise, I think, on 13 June 1483, and I've always thought that is a critical moment for trying to assess whether the norms of political life have been stretched too far. I always think they must have been, just as I think that Charles Ross's piece of evidence, not given to us here, of the way Anthony Woodville, Earl Rivers in March 1483 chooses as an arbitrator, in a land dispute in East Anglia, Richard, duke of Gloucester. We could say that someone as involved in Yorkist political life as Anthony Woodville is also taken by surprise by Richard's arrest of him at Stony Stratford in late April 1483, because he's gone out of his way to bring the prince to meet his uncle. This is not a direct route. And so two very real, what would be the American equivalent of such experienced politicians? Or rather, William, Lord Hastings in 1483 is like Harold MacMillan. And then the murder itself or whatever, that too – although we talked a little earlier about infants, murdered infants, or whether it was actual murder or people beginning to believe that the uncle had killed the nephews – breaks some boundaries.

Griffiths It appears that in 1483 the parameters are still moving outward in brutality.

Richmond I'd use another gesture or model here, not of pulling out but going from one level to the next. I think, somehow, a slippage – we use all these jargon words – a sort of slippage from one to another. There's a slippage in 1459–60 and then there's another in 1483.

Richmond Well, the civil servants won't have it, will they? Either they go into exile, these Yorkist administrators; they either go into exile with Henry Tudor, or they lie low.

Griffiths Well, do they? I don't know if they do stay.

Richmond This is what I'm trying to suggest. Alas, I can't come up with other than a varied response.

Griffiths Varied, yes, but the characteristic of Richard's reign is that they do *not* stay.

Richmond Yes, I think there's a trickle away; this is what makes it unusual.

Guth May I introduce another element here. There is a sense of permanency, and councillors are very much part of a régime. They are there for policy; they are there particularly as informers, as people who not only carry information from the country into the centre, but who carry it back out from the centre; they are people who provide part of their régime's policy, the equivalent of modern-day cabinet ministers and all of their hangers-on. But they're not civil servants; they're not part of that sort of lower-echelon or local stable, the folks who really have a commitment to government, to keep the basic civility in society. Those are the ones that we have to identify. And I'm the first to confess that all I did was throw that out without having a long list of saying, 'these are the people from 1460 to 1500 who qualify as civil servants; these are the ones who qualify as councillors, and these are the ones who are just sort of interested in the centre.' I do think there's a difference between councillors and civil servants.

Blanchard [Suggests an inventory be made of the 'survivors' who made it through all the reigns intact, looking for commonalities.]

Richmond These occasions are always intended to encourage work.

Blanchard [Suggests Ludford as a seminal experience for the young, impressionable Richard, based on a piece of artistic licence in Kendall, *Richard III* (New York, 1955), p. 37, where he says Cecily and the boys awaited the Lancastrians at the market cross and then notes in the back of the book that this is a conjecture on his part.]

Richmond But isn't Richard in Warwick's household?

Miller What part does betrayal, changing sides, play in this? You're bringing up Osbert's brother-in-law, Trollope, and he betrayed Warwick, shifting sides, and vengeance would seem to play into the brutality. He changed sides.

Richmond I think that may well apply very much to Warwick, just looking at things very briefly and characterizing as nasty the things going on at Calais; I think vengeance may well be a motor here. But, I mean, again, it's always this angle of vision, isn't it? It's often said that disloyalty, for example, or betrayal is a feature of the Wars of the Roses, but equally, if your angle is towards loyalty and so on, then you find plenty of examples of that too, as Ian Arthurson has shown in an article in the *Ricardian*, a very important paper, stressing how we should look at some of the people who were loyal. Unless you are a quantifier and want to say here are 2.6 loyalists and 1.987 betrayers, but then I'm not a quantifier and I don't think you can ever do that with that sort of thing, so once again it's these terrible variables, isn't it?

Guth This brings us back to the point of loyalty and the elasticity or inelasticity of loyalty and the question of what are people still prepared to be loyal to? How far do you go in your behaviour? That becomes a real question: the popular element is very important.

Richmond That's why for a long time I've wanted to see Bosworth as the – what is it? – hubris or nemesis, or whatever, for Richard of his behaviour in June 1483. I say 'I want to see that': that's the moral necessity argument.

Guth It's a minor redemption of Shakespeare: God finally had had enough.

Reeves Ralph Griffiths can offer some comparative instances of how people remained loyal, and why, as Henry VI was obviously failing; what sort of degree of tolerance extended there.

Griffiths They are distinctly different. The degree of tolerance was very high for Henry VI. He wasn't a pretty sort of king, I suppose, but he must have stirred an awful lot of people – he evidently stirred the chroniclers. What alters your parameters a little is the Battle of St Albans in 1455. In that battle the king was shot and wounded in the neck. All the chroniclers mention that but they never say who did it, as if it seemed a major turning-point. Nothing happened to Henry VI, one way or another; his politics were at most criticized, but nothing comparable to that. And then afterwards, you get used to it, you're willing to go a little further; then you say, well it's hopeless, he's ill, we can go a step further because by 1460 . . .

Reeves But then in June of 1483 there's just this quantum leap to new levels . . .

Griffiths Well, there is a whole new level in 1483 . . .

Reeves But you get it in very tiny increments . . .

Griffiths But in 1483 there *is* a major change, isn't there? They depose, they remove the king; he may be an infant, but they've had child kings in the past, and there's been no significant problem. But in 1483 opinion is prepared to accept the deposition of the king. That does strike me as what brought things to such a pitch.

Guth The parallels between 1483 and Watergate are very interesting. The Weekend of the Long Knives: Nixon finally is up against it and he has to dismiss Archibald Cox; he has already lost Ruckelshaus; and all of these people who have great stature at large in terms of their individual political integrity are suddenly being tossed to the wolves by the leader! – the leader! – the person to whom we owe fealty. Homage! And so I think that's dramatic, and again in terms of just concentrated two or three days of events; to me the whole thing turns on that in terms of again people saying, 'you've gone far enough'. These are respectable men. These are individuals and they were dropping like that, as Nixon was firing them and had finally to go down as low as Bork to get someone to do the dirty work. At that point, bells were ringing in most people's heads, so that there is that sort of bang.

Richmond That would certainly fit my interpretation of Buckingham's rebellion, not that it's mine, that the bells had rung for all those key household men of Edward IV's reign whose allegiance or homage principally had been, once Edward IV had died (though there's no technical or legal changeover), to

Edward V. To answer Ralph Griffiths's point, I think they're all taken by surprise, so much so in June – this is a wonderful orchestrated coup in June 1483 – but once the rumour or maybe more, the disappearance or the killing of the princes, and once they had collected themselves, that's what the rising of 1483 is about. They had had enough. The bells have rung and that's it. And one interpretation may be that Richard dealt with that, and dealt with that very skilfully. But this is where I think recent work has shown that there is a continuing trickle away, as Ralph Griffiths expressed it, and once you get to Bosworth, that king just doesn't have the support a king should or would normally anticipate. Whatever the nature of the battle and whether it's touch-and-go, it shouldn't have been touch-and-go. He should have been able to win hands down there, despite the Scots and French.

Morgan The notion of Bosworth as a kind of restorative end to the period of instability doesn't sit quite easily with notions of civil society. We are thinking of notions of pragmatism rather than of moral neatness. And the moral neatness has to be related as much to what would have been in the minds of the people: like when More sits down to write his account of all this, the imagery is about healing the wounds, about the return of stability and order.

Richmond But you see, Thomas More can't finish that book. That may be because he wants to see things, just as I'm wanting to see things. Oh! That's very interesting! Very interesting! Because that desire to see things as I wish to see them, that is in moral necessity terms, black and white and so on. It's often said, and it may be true, that Thomas More, in writing this extraordinary book (after all, it is the first history book, etcetera), when he comes to examine contemporary politics, or he's looking back at, say, the equivalent of Nixon and such like – my God, it's all *grey!* Just as I am coming to this conclusion by looking at these councillors, I can't come to it by looking at these councillors: it's all a *fuzzy grey area.* That's not the black and white. So what does Thomas More do? He goes and writes *Utopia* where he can figure these things out in black and white.

Griffiths Maybe that's the trouble with Edwardian England: it created only grey people. We've talked about people who feel a sense of loyalty no matter what, but there are increasingly large numbers of people, up to 1483, who step aside, don't want to be involved, but in '83, feel that they will rebel.

Richmond Neutrality is not enough any more.

Griffiths They will not stand aside any longer. These are the people to a large extent whom Henry Tudor relies on. They are the people who re-emerged, so to speak, loyal, to restore the crown.

Richmond You know, we're getting dangerously back to theories of all this that date from a hundred years ago. But that's no bad thing anymore.

Guth Let me just add one final thing. Of all the alternatives, assuming he survived the battle, could Richard III have had the same fate, after 1485, that Richard Nixon did after Watergate? If Richard had lived, could he then have become a kind of *eminence grise*, someone who rehabilitates himself, who becomes respectable again as the seer who had a vision, learning, writing the right books and maybe the right definitive book against More's, that More had received in Morton's household. It boggles the mind. I don't think there was any opportunity for Richard to live after 1485. The norms would not have allowed this.

Michalove It strikes me that he would have been the type that, had he escaped Bosworth, he would have tried to come back again, not sit off somewhere writing his memoirs.

Guth I was just thinking: this has been the most fascinating intellectual catharsis I have had! I mean, just the chemistry that has gone on, and I think again that what Sharon Michalove has done in bringing everyone together – it may have been a small group – but it has *worked*. It worked from day one. This to me has just been – and I can't think of a better – the way you really want a seminar to go on and on and on.

Richmond This is a confession that I'd only make under these circumstances. The very first sort of public lecture I gave (leaving aside the lecture I gave at school on the history of jazz, which is another story and I'll tell you another time), leaving that aside as a sort of proto-public lecture, the first public lecture I gave was on Richard III when I was in – whatever year you call it – the final year or senior year, and that was, oh, a terrible lecture, all taken from Murray Kendall, really. But it was a defence of Richard III; it was in praise of Richard III. That was in 1958, and I think the whole of my life subsequently has been trying to raze the memory of doing that. It seems a long time ago. But I have in the past therefore stood up for him, so I thought in these circles you'd like that – even though I was then a very raw youth.

Blanchard I think it's very interesting that now you're raising the possibility that 'Richard III is coming out better than I thought over the past thirty years . . .'.

Richmond Are you quoting there?

Blanchard '. . . if fellows like Russell were willing to make an accommodation'. And moreover, 'My God, they're all grey'.

6

'THOSE WERE THE DAYS': A YORKIST PEDIGREE ROLL[1]

Philip Morgan

Of what, one wonders, did the guests of the elderly Yorkist bureaucrat, Sir John Wood, talk over dinner at Rivers Hall near Boxted, Essex, in the summer of 1484? The household included Wood's wife, Margaret Lewkenor; his bailiff, the Lollard William Sweeting; Sir Thomas Lewkenor, bound over to reside with his brother-in-law after his lengthy resistance at Bodiam Castle during the rebellion of 1483; Sir Thomas's wife, Jane, the widow of Sir John Young, late a grocer and mayor of London; and her mother, Joan Boughton. Andrew Hope believes, and has argued persuasively, that William Sweeting used the summer to convert Lady Jane, and perhaps also her mother, to Lollardy.[2] These were unsafe conversations which had their final fatal effects in 1494 when the eighty-year-old mother, Joan Boughton, was burnt at Smithfield and her daughter likewise stigmatized as having 'the smell of an heretic'.[3]

But, it was the men's discourse which may then have seemed the more perilous. Speaker in Edward IV's last parliament, appointed treasurer after the king's death and confirmed in office by Richard III, Sir John Wood, like so many

---

[1] The original lecture given at the Urbana conference was then already promised but not published; see note 7. I am grateful to the editors for their indulgence in allowing me to submit another paper here in its place. I have tried to mimic the style and context of the original occasion.

[2] All of this is from Andrew Hope, 'The Lady and the Bailiff: Lollardy among the Gentry in Yorkist and Early Tudor England', in Margaret Aston and Colin Richmond (eds), *Lollardy and the Gentry in the Later Middle Ages* (Stroud, 1997), pp. 250–77. I am grateful to Dr Hope for allowing me to read a draft of his article in advance of publication.

[3] *Ibid.*, pp. 250–1, 259–60.

other civil servants, had made his accommodation with the new régime. Lewkenor, summoned to Edward V's coronation and created a Knight of the Bath at Richard III's, was less inured to the sudden shift which marked the usurpation and was quickly disenchanted. His rebellion in 1483 has about it the air of obduracy, as his later petition for pardon – appealing as 'a sorrowful and repentaunt subgett' to Richard's 'princely pité' – exhibits the eternal fear of being in harm's way without the necessary papers.[4] Neither man was to survive the summer, both perhaps victims of epidemic illness.[5] Were they then during this time more often in each other's company than in that of their wives, in this household of aged men and women, their younger charges and servants? And if in this they resembled that model Christian household described by St Paul in his letter to Titus, did they, while failing to follow the Pauline advice on the avoidance of heresy, also fail to heed his admonition to 'avoid foolish questions and genealogies'.[6]

I have argued that an early report of the murder of Edward V, circulating in the autumn of 1483, and concluding a Lancastrian lineage history, belonged to the circle of the Lewkenor family.[7] The king-list calls him *Edwardus quintus infans* and notes that he was killed and his body 'drowned', *submersum fuit*, on 26 June 1483. The echoes are of other reports of drowning in *The Great Chronicle*, and of later traditions, notably William Rastell's *The Pastime of the People* (1529) and the 1557 edition of Thomas More's *History of King Richard III*, that the body was cast into the Thames contained in a chest.[8] In 1483 it was surely the word

---

[4] The petition is printed by Colin Richmond, '1485 and all that, or what was going on at the Battle of Bosworth', in P.W. Hammond (ed.), *Richard III: Loyalty, Lordship and Law* (London, 1986), p. 198 n. 60.

[5] Andrew Hope, 'The Lady and the Bailiff', p. 258.

[6] Titus 3, 9. The preacher's text on the Sunday on which I commenced to write this piece.

[7] Philip Morgan, 'The Death of Edward V and the Rebellion of 1483', *Historical Research*, 68 (1995), 229–32.

[8] A.H. Thomas and I.D. Thornley (eds), *The Great Chronicle of London* (London, 1938), pp. 236–7; A. Hanham, *Richard III and His Early Historians, 1483–1535* (Oxford, 1975), p. 104. I owe the reference to Sir Thomas More to Dr Steven Gunn.

infans,[9] Edward the 'child' king, which resonated. For civil servants like Sir John Wood, as indeed for St Paul, these were – though for different reasons – indeed foolish questions. Paul had sent the same advice to Timothy, this time glossing over his reasons, 'Neither give heed to fables and endless genealogies, which minister questions, rather than godly edifying'.[10] What sustained the actions of men like Sir John Wood seems, like bureaucrats everywhere, to have been their reading of the material world, rather than their moral attitude to the murder of children. The central administration, we are told, survived almost unchanged. As the women sought godly edifying, was it this then that engaged the two men during that summer, as it surely informed the rebellion of 1483?

Politics, foolish or serious, led some men to think of genealogies. The Manchester townsman, George Manchester, did so in his will of 20 October 1483. It is idiosyncratically dated 'the fyrst yere of the regne of kyng Richard the thyrd after the conquest when he raysed hys realme agaynes the Duke of Bokyngham', and in its terms he was prepared, if his three sons had no male issue, for his lands to pass to 'Thurstan of Manchester my brother and hys heres male laghfully begottyn or bastard so that it be in the name'.[11] He at least was prepared to stand up for the bastards in his own family. Of course, there was no telling when and where thoughts of genealogy might arise, nor the form which they might take.[12] The single folio containing two king-lists, within which the notice of Edward V's murder appears, is a modest affair, but belongs to a class

---

[9] Its use in the Latin Vulgate is almost wholly restricted to the newly born, although in later usage it is applied to minors in wardship. Du Cange, *Glossarium mediæ et infirmæ latinitatis* (Paris, 1938), iv, 351–2; R.E. Latham, *Revised Medieval Latin Word-List* (London, 1965), p. 247.

[10] 1 Timothy 1, 4.

[11] William E.A. Axon, 'A Manchester Will of the Fifteenth Century', in *Echoes of Old Lancashire* (1899), pp. 106–10. It is there said to have been deposited at the Peel Park Museum, Salford. Mr Cross, the Salford City Archivist, tells me it has migrated to Manchester Central Reference Library.

[12] In 1478 the birth of Sir Roger Townshend I's son was noted in the margin of the family's sheep accounts. C.E. Moreton, *The Townshends and their World: Gentry, Law, and Land in Norfolk, c. 1450–1551* (Oxford, 1992), p. 20.

now called the chronicle or pedigree roll. In an early attempt to explain the genre, for which in 1872 he had coined the term 'feudal manual', Thomas Wright, the great antiquarian, wrote:

> In the baronial hall, after dinner, when the lord of the manor was seated with his guests and followers around his table, songs were sung, and historical as well as romantic poetry was chanted, often connected with old questions of family or with political movements of the time; and to decide these or assist in the discussion, the head of the family would bring forth his historical roll.[13]

Attention to the family and its genealogy might, of course, also fall within the compass of private devotion, in marginal additions routinely made to the calendar of the saints, or added to the contents of commonplace books. The Book of Hours belonging to Sir Thomas Lewkenor's father, inherited by his brother, was carefully annotated with such family obits. It also contained a souvenir of a pilgrimage to Bromholm and an image of the side wound of Christ with its measure, both expressions of an orthodox piety.[14] It is impossible to know of what they spoke at Rivers Hall, nor any of the details of what might be called the home life of Sir John Wood. Endeavouring to place these random actions and records, random of course only in their survival, results in a search for moral acts and a moral context. It would be useful to see Sir Thomas Lewkenor's resistance in 1483 and the labelling of Edward V as a child as, in one sense, moral acts. Did the moral context within which the genealogy of the kings of England and the murder of Edward V were discussed also render Lady Jane and her mother all the more receptive to William Sweeting's conversion? Certainly Andrew Hope's careful search unearthed no pedigree for Lollardy.

---

[13] Thomas Wright, *Feudal Manuals of English History* (London, 1872), p. ix.

[14] Andrew Hope, 'The Lady and the Bailiff', p. 258; London, Lambeth Palace Library, MS 545, ff. 185r, 78v. The family obits are given *in extenso* in M.R. James, *Descriptive Catalogue of the MSS. in the Library of Lambeth Palace*. The cult of the *mensura vulneris* is discussed in Eamon Duffy, *The Stripping of the Altars: Traditional Religion in England, 1400–1580* (London, 1992), p. 245.

Howbeit, it is clear that another contemporary pedigree roll belonged to a patently amoral if as yet anonymous household.

Latin MS 113 in the John Rylands Library is an illuminated pedigree roll of eleven unequal membranes measuring 14 in by 2 ft and 6 ins.[15] Its contemporary heading describes it thus: *hic incipiunt cronice bone et compendiose de regibus anglie a noe usque in hunc diem*, 'To this day'. A later, possibly eighteenth-century, hand added *usque ad annum 1484* to a new title. There are stylized portrait medallions of twenty-nine kings of England from Brutus to Richard III, three others, of the queens of Edward II, Edward III and Edward IV, and medallions with golden crowns for Richard II, Henry IV, Henry V and Henry VI. The roll ends with a medallion containing a golden crown for Henry VII. M.R. James's description is characteristically enticing: after dating it as 'after 1485', he observes that 'the text ends with a series of circles containing notices of the children of Edward IV. Preparations were seemingly made for carrying on the genealogy.' When were the days in which the roll was compiled? And how, in this presumably grander household, were matters of royal genealogy discussed?

Dining room or school room? Margaret Gibson wrote, 'The medieval poster – or its near equivalent – was the roll: a dozen or more sheets of parchment sewn together to be hung vertically, perhaps in the schoolroom'.[16] Was this history at a glance, the whole thing enhanced with pictures? Such edifying narratives, often with denser texts, were displayed in public as *tabulae*, histories on boards for visitors to churches.[17] However, having adopted a format, bureaucratic in origin, the readers of pedigree rolls surely followed a similar etiquette, one hand rolling,

---

[15] Manchester, John Rylands University Library, Latin MS 113; M.R. James, *A Descriptive Catalogue of the Latin Manuscripts in the John Rylands Library at Manchester* (2 vols, Manchester, 1921), pp. 199–200.

[16] *Medieval Manuscripts on Merseyside* (Centre for Medieval Studies, Liverpool, 1993), pp. 32–3. Gordon Hall Gerould, 'A Text of Merlin's Prophecies', *Speculum*, xxiii (1948), 102, characterized an example from the library at Princeton as 'ready reference as well as the education of the young'.

[17] Antonia Gransden, *Historical Writing in England II. c. 1307 to the Early Sixteenth Century* (London, 1982), p. 495; Colin Richmond, 'Hand and mouth: information gathering and use in England in the later middle ages', *Journal of Historical Sociology*, 1 (1988), 246–7; *idem*, *The Paston Family in the Fifteenth Century: Fastolf's will* (Cambridge, 1996), p. 78 n. 90.

the other unrolling to leave a middle section for reading – altogether a more intimate, perhaps often a domestic, environment. Lordly and knightly families, used to administrative records, read their history and romance like manorial accounts.

The Rylands pedigree roll adopts a conventional Yorkist attitude to the descent of the English crown. The true line of royal descent is throughout shown by a thick red band and, after the death of Edward III, embraces the claims through the female line of the earls of March. Both Edmund, earl of March (d. 1425) and Richard, duke of York (d. 1460) are described as 'true heirs to England'; the accession of Edward IV, a 'true Brutus', is said to have restored the title and just crown. The line ends with the portrait roundel of Richard III, although the red band continues below and was presumably intended for continuation. The earlier kingship of Richard II is removed to the left-hand side, that of the Lancastrian kings to the right with their descent marked now by a thinner green band. It ends with the demise without heirs of Edward, prince of Wales (d. 1471), 'the only son of king Henry killed in battle'. The children of Edward IV are dealt with in similar fashion. No title is accorded to Edward V, who is said simply to have 'died without heirs in youth' – the telling difference then between a young man and a child – and Duke Richard is said likewise to have died without heirs. Of other children, only Elizabeth is noted, as also is her marriage to Henry VII. No further issue is shown although four lines descend to the foot of the membrane. The accession of Henry VII is accommodated on the roll by the addition of a thick black line in the right margin which traces his descent straight to the time of Henry V, to 'Owen Tyder', a chamber servant, 'married' to the widowed Katherine de Valois, which goes to show no doubt that one should never pass up the chance of sleeping with a queen.[18]

Epitomes of the reigns of kings are added at intervals to the genealogy. They add but a little to the Yorkist claims evident from the descent. Recognition of Richard, duke of York's claim to be Henry VI's heir apparent through Mortimer

---

[18] *Owen Tyder unus servitorum in camera cum ista domina Katerina ipsa relicta sustitavit super eam proles ut sequitur.*

as right heir to Richard II is attributed to 1451. Edward III's claims to the French crown through the female line are emphasized (one line rewritten over an erasure), as are his martial exploits and those of Edward, the Black Prince, and Henry V. Henry V's particular attention to the cult of Richard II, his return of the body from Langley to Westminster, his support for the fund which gave alms to the poor on the anniversary of his death, and Henry's willingness to seek papal absolution for the Lancastrian usurpation are praised. Henry VI's piety is noted and the loss of all the lands in France is matter-of-factly ascribed to his little care for warlike interests. All of this emphasizes a knightly readership for the roll.

And it does seem to have been a voracious readership in the fifteenth century. In 1872 Thomas Wright observed that chronicle rolls had 'hitherto attracted little attention among antiquaries' and printed six examples. In the thirteenth century they combine Biblical texts from Peter of Poitiers, British history from Geoffrey of Monmouth, the traditional pedigrees of Anglo-Saxon kings and epitomes of more recent history.[19] Sydney Anglo has listed forty-six examples from the reigns of Henry VI and Edward IV alone.[20] Many of these later examples are unashamedly propagandist. British Library Additional MS 18268A shows Edward IV, heir of the kings of Britain and the Plantagenets, fulfilling the prophecy of Merlin as the white dragon in his defeat of Henry VI, the last heir of the Anglo-Saxon kings, as the red dragon.[21] Also interesting are those lordly families who began to add their own lineages to the margins of royal genealogies, as did the earls of Northumberland shortly after 1485.[22] Any Tom, Dick or Harry might be king now.

---

[19] M.T. Clanchy, *From Memory to Written Record. England, 1066–1307* (London, 1979), p. 112 and pl. xiii; W.H. Monroe, '13th and early 14th century illustrated genealogical manuscripts in roll and codex: Peter of Poitiers' Compendium, universal histories and chronicles of the kings of England' (unpublished Ph.D. thesis, Courtauld Institute, London University, 1990).

[20] Sydney Anglo, 'The British History in Early Tudor Propaganda', *Bulletin of the John Rylands Library*, 44 (1961), 17–48.

[21] Michael Powell Siddons, 'Welsh Pedigree Rolls', *The National Library of Wales Journal*, 29 (1996), 3–4.

[22] Oxford, Bodleian Library Exhibition, 3 February–3 May 1997, 'Land and Lineage: the world of the nobility and gentry in England, 1500–1700', no. 20: Bodl. Rolls 5.

The Rylands pedigree roll falls into this final category and allows us to consider the three questions of the roll's authorship, its date and its provenance. The crucial passage is contained in the epitome of the reign of Richard III. It commences with a note of the coronation and moves to a record of a great parliament held at Westminster in the second year of the reign at which, for default of a male heir, Richard is said to have adopted John, earl of Lincoln as his heir apparent and, with the general assent of the nobility, to have had it widely proclaimed. Thereafter, Richard is said to have reigned for almost three years and to have been buried at Leicester. The final genealogy, to the left of the royal trunk as that of Henry VII lay to the right, is of the children of John, duke of Suffolk (d. 1492) and Elizabeth, daughter of Richard, duke of York. The medallion of John, earl of Lincoln partially overlaps the central royal trunk like the medallions of other earlier Mortimer claimants from Lionel, duke of Clarence onwards.

The death of Prince Edward in April 1484 had left Richard III without an heir. Hitherto, John Rous's story that the king initially regarded the ten-year old Edward, earl of Warwick as his heir before recognizing the earl of Lincoln has been treated with some scepticism, at least as far as formal recognition was concerned.[23] However, this is precisely what is asserted by the Rylands pedigree roll which must therefore belong to the circle of the de la Poles. Its evidence is questionable in some details. Richard III summoned no parliament after that of January 1484 and, if proclamations were made in the summer of 1484 (at the same time as significant grants to the earl),[24] they cannot have originated in a parliamentary assembly. Whether John Rous was reporting de la Pole propaganda or whether the Rylands roll simply confirms his own report of the king's nomination of an heir is probably not important. Here, at the foot of the roll, we are among the men who would be kings.

---

[23] John Rous, *Historia Regum Angliae* (Oxford, 1745), pp. 217–8; Charles Ross, *Richard III* (London, 1981), pp. 158–9; Rosemary Horrox, *Richard III: A Study of Service* (Cambridge, 1989), p. 299.

[24] J.A.F. Thomson, 'John de la Pole, duke of Suffolk', *Speculum*, 54 (1979), 536.

The dating of the roll is problematic. Six children of the duke of Suffolk are named, John, earl of Lincoln and the five younger brothers, Edmund, Edward, Humphrey, William and Richard. Of John, earl of Lincoln it is said that 'he was killed in battle against Henry VII'. No titles are accorded to the others. Edmund is said to have died without issue; an addition in the same hand further reports that this was because 'he was imprisoned by Henry VII and beheaded by his son'. Edward is reported simply to have died without heirs, Humphrey to have been an ecclesiastic, *ecclesiasticus vir et sacerdos fieri onerint*, and William to have been imprisoned by Henry VII and to have died without heirs. The fate of Richard de la Pole is unrecorded; the roll has a hole at this point. There are no dates for any of these events.

Edward de la Pole, generally seen as the second son, but here said to be the third, is thought to have died before 1485. The eldest son, John, earl of Lincoln, was killed at the battle of Stoke on 16 June 1487. Edmund, here the second son, was imprisoned in the Tower after 1506; William, the fifth son, from 1502. The former was executed in 1513, but William is now assumed to have survived until 1539. Humphrey de la Pole, rector of Hingham, Norfolk, died before 15 February 1513. Richard de la Pole was killed at the battle of Pavia in 1525.[25]

What then are the possible dates for the commissioning of the roll? Although the chronology of de la Pole deaths would suggest a date as late as 1513, perhaps even 1539, I do not see the roll as a consoling elegy for a decayed de la Pole servant. The emphasis upon John de la Pole's designation as Richard III's heir in 1484 and his continuing and realistic ambitions even after Henry VII's accession seem to me to be the immediate context for the roll. The addition of Henry VII's kingship and the disparaging description of Owain Tudor look like additions to an original design. Thereafter, Humphrey de la Pole's religious status is precisely defined; he is an ecclesiastic but not yet a priest. He was ordained an acolyte in 1491 and was rector of Leverington, Cambridgeshire, by 1500. The reference to Edmund's imprisonment and execution is an addition. Finally, Richard de la Pole

---

[25] G.E. Cokayne, *The Complete Peerage* (13 vols, London, 1910–59), xii, pt. i, 21–5. The pedigree roll provides no confirmation of the existence of another putative son, Geoffrey.

is oddly described as the second-born son of Duke John, an assertion that possibly made sense only after Edmund's capture in 1506. Together these observations seem to point, not to a single moment of composition but to a continuous programme over perhaps ten or fifteen years, between about 1484 and about 1500.

On whose dinner table (or school-room wall) was the de la Pole bad news gradually accumulated? The illumination on the roll is not English (nor the penmanship, thought M.R. James, who posited a Rouen workshop) but this does not help much since almost everybody went abroad for their pictures.[26] John de la Pole's presence in the Low Countries in 1487, and other brothers' absences from England after 1500, do not seem significant in this context. That household in the end eludes us, as also does the identity of the survivor who could say of the de la Pole search for the crown, 'those were the days'.

---

[26] Colin Richmond, 'The Visual Culture of Fifteenth-Century England', in A.J. Pollard (ed.), *The Wars of the Roses* (London, 1995), pp. 187–8.

7

The Education of Aristocratic Women in Fifteenth-century England

Sharon D. Michalove

According to Christine de Pizan in *The Book of the Three Virtues*, in order to carry out her responsibilities, a lady had to have a good, and appropriate, education.

> The men usually are at court or in distant countries. So the ladies will have responsibilities for managing their property, their revenues, and their lands. In order for such a woman to act with good judgment, she must know the yearly income from her estate. She must manage it so well that by conferring with her husband, her gentle words and good counsel will lead to their agreement to follow a plan for the state that their revenues permit. . . . The lady or demoiselle must be well informed about the rights of domain of fiefs and secondary fiefs, about contributions, the lord's rights of harvest, shared crops, and all other rights of possession and the customs both local and foreign. . . . She should know how to manage accounts and should attend to them often, also superintending her agents' treatment of her tenants and men.[1]

How did women obtain the education that Christine de Pizan thought so necessary for an aristocratic woman? Defining education for gentry and noblewomen in late medieval England is very difficult because the records are

---

[1] Christine de Pizan, *A Medieval Woman's Mirror of Honor: The Treasure of the City of Ladies*, tr. C.C. Willard, ed. M.P. Cosman (New York, 1989), pp. 170–1.

allusive, scattered and incomplete. Because the sources do not explicitly describe this education, other methods must be used to uncover women's interests in education and the types of education they might have had.[2] While educational theorists in the twentieth century look at education as a way to produce a far-reaching transformation of society, in late medieval England education was closely allied to the maintenance of the social structure. The type of education available to an individual varied by class and by gender. Aristocrats – male and female – were taught to rule, whether it was over a parish, a bishopric, a household or a kingdom. While it may seem obvious that men needed to be able to rule their social inferiors and their own families, women also needed to be able to rule others – especially their children and their servants. As Christine de Pizan pointed out, married women whose husbands held land were also frequently responsible for overseeing estate matters when their spouses were away at war or at court.[3] With both justice and court patronage principally located in London, aristocratic men were frequently away from home. Women would need the same knowledge as their husbands if they were to manage the day-to-day affairs of the household. Sociologist Christopher Hurn defines education as the 'more or less

[2] Books about medieval and Renaissance women have proliferated but discussions of women's education are still somewhat sparse. Some studies that provide background include the essays in P. Labalme (ed.), *Beyond Their Sex: Learned Women of the European Past* (New York, 1980); Margaret Hallissy, *Clean Maids, True Wives, Steadfast Widows: Chaucer's Women and Medieval Codes of Conduct* (Westport, Conn., 1993); R.M. Warnicke, *Women of the English Renaissance and Reformation* (Westport, Conn., 1983); S.W. Hull, *Chaste, Silent & Obedient: English Books for Women, 1475–1640* (San Marino, Calif., 1982), and *Women According to Men: The World of Tudor-Stuart Women* (Walnut Creek, Calif., 1996). Margaret King's *Women of the Renaissance* (Chicago, Ill., 1986) has some useful information but the book must be used with caution except when looking at Italy. Books that are primarily concerned with Renaissance women, have a literary emphasis and take thought-provoking approaches include P.J. Benson, *The Invention of the Renaissance Woman: The Challenge of Female Independence in the Literature and Thought of Italy and England* (University Park, Penn., 1992), and L. Woodbridge, *Women and the English Renaissance: Literature and the Nature of Womankind, 1540–1620* (Urbana, Ill., 1984).

[3] Christine de Pizan's book, *Le Livre des Trois Vertus*, is a manual to help upper-class women learn how to meet these various demands. Most manuals meant to guide women in running a household were written by men, such as le Chevalier de la Tour-Landry and le Ménagier de Paris.

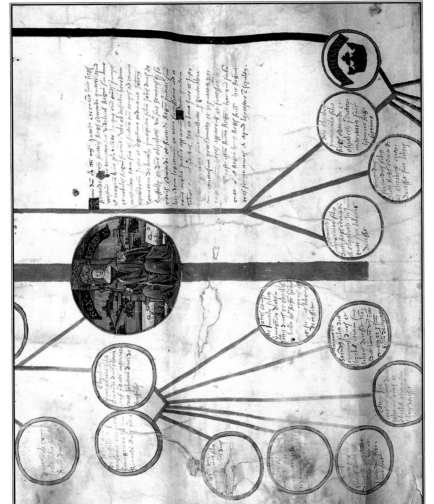

Plate 1

Plate 2

Plate 3

Plate Captions

Plate 1
The Men who would be Kings. The foot of a pedigree roll commissioned while Richard III was king and including the crown's putative heirs, members of the de la Pole family to the left, with John, earl of Lincoln's medallion brushing the trunk of royal descent. Edward IV's murdered children are shown to the right. The immediate success of the rank outsider, Henry VII, was accommodated by a sombre black line to the right and his marriage to Elizabeth of York. (Manchester, John Rylands University Library, Latin MS 113.)

Plate 2
Richard III. A medallion portrait of the king, the true heir of his brother, Edward IV, commissioned in the following of John, earl of Lincoln after 1484. Richard's 'line' continues to the foot of the roll, but ends abruptly. (Manchester, John Rylands University Library, Latin MS 113.)

Plate 3
Edward IV and his queen, Elizabeth Woodville. Portrait medallions on a pedigree roll commissioned during the reign of Richard III. The king and queen are shown significantly turned and gesturing to the lineage of Richard, duke of York and its connections to the de la Pole family which occupy the left side of the roll. (Manchester, John Rylands University Library, Latin MS 113.)

All these illustrations are reproduced by courtesy of the Director and University Librarian, the John Rylands University of Manchester.

deliberate process of transmitting the culture of the adult world to the young. . . .
In this sense, all societies educate the young, whether or not the societies possess
those institutions we call schools.'[4] It is this socialization process that is the
hallmark of aristocratic education in late medieval England.

Any discussion of education must deal with the subject of literacy. Literacy is a
particularly difficult aspect of education with which to grapple because we
associate literacy as much with writing as with reading – an association that was
not central to late medieval conceptions of literacy. The ability to read was not
tied to the ability to write. The materials of writing – parchment and quills –
made the exercise difficult. Reading was also more identified with speaking since
most reading was done aloud, in groups, rather than as the solitary occupation it
has become in modern society.[5] M.T. Clanchy suggests that '[a]lthough the
average medieval reader had been taught to form the letters of the alphabet with
a stylus on a writing tablet, he would not necessarily have felt confident about
penning a letter or a charter on parchment'.[6] One difficulty is that, in modern
society, full participation is extremely difficult without some skill in both reading
and writing. However, medieval people had many ways of acquiring information.
If they could not read or write, they usually had access to someone who could
read to them and write for them. People who could not read or write could still
participate in lettered society. An important example is Margery Kempe.
Although a member of the merchant class of the provincial town of Bishop's (now
King's) Lynn rather than a member of the aristocracy, she is important in the
discussion about what constituted literate society in fifteenth-century England.
Margery was definitely illiterate, as she mentions in her *Book*,[7] but priests read to
her and she was very familiar not only with the Bible but also with contemporary
devotional texts such as Walter Hilton's *The Scale of Perfection* and Richard Rolle's

    [4] C.J. Hurn, *The Limits and Possibilities of Schooling* (Boston, 1993), p. 4.

    [5] M.T. Clanchy, *From Memory to Written Record: England, 1066–1307* (Cambridge, Mass., 1980),
p. 183.

    [6] Clanchy, p. 183.

    [7] B.A. Windeatt (trans.), *The Book of Margery Kempe* (London, 1985), p. 16.

Incendium Amoris.[8] While written records had become more common, society still relied on memory and an oral culture for the transmission of information. Margery Kempe's ability to produce her *Book*, by dictation to a scribe, who was also a priest, shows the close interconnection between literate and non-literate society in late medieval England. Less of society was marginalized by a lack of literate skills than is true today. A narrow definition of literacy is merely a reflection of our own preoccupations rather than a window into another world. As Rosemary O'Day points out,

> Both reading and writing were regarded in much the same light as cobbling, tanning or thatching – they were specialist skills specific to certain occupations. Even were we to prove that actual literacy levels were low, this would not imply necessarily that the population was 'uneducated'. Rather, it would demonstrate that reading and writing were not considered essential skills required in the transmission of culture or opinion or in the business of daily life.[9]

The likelihood that women of the aristocratic and gentry classes could read is high. Women in the families of ordinary gentry and bourgeoisie seem often to have been able to read. Joyce, Lady Tiptoft, the mother of John Tiptoft, earl of Worcester, carefully instructed her son at home, both in moral precepts and in literature.[10] She may have given the same education to her daughters – Philippa, Joanna, Joyce, and another who was a nun and whose name was not recorded.[11]

Some women could probably write, if not with the practised ease of clerks. This was certainly true of women like Margaret Paston, who could read and

---

[8] *The Book of Margery Kempe*, p. 9.

[9] Rosemary O'Day, *Education and Society, 1500–1800: The Social Foundations of Education in Early Modern Britain* (London, 1982), p. 13.

[10] R.J. Mitchell, *John Tiptoft (1427–1470)* (London, 1938), p. 12.

[11] *Ibid.*, p. 11.

who could at least sign her name, but who dictated her letters to clerks. Her daughter-in-law, Margery Brews, could certainly write, but usually chose not to, even when writing intimate letters such as the valentine she sent to her suitor and future husband, John Paston III. On the other hand, Eleanor Townshend, not only read the estate accounts, which were kept in English rather than Latin, but kept her own book, 'a "Boke off certeyn Bargeyns"', in which a clerk recorded the sales she made of agricultural goods and the leases she negotiated.[12]

Women played a crucial role in managing the household, which was more like a business than a modern household. However, while women were daily proving their ability, they were being stereotyped in contemporary popular culture that was part of an antifeminist tradition. A strong strain of misogyny runs through medieval literature, denigrating women's ability, morality and integrity. The perfect wife was said to be patient Griselda who put up with all manner of outrages to prove herself worthy. The *fabliaux* attacked women as lewd and unfaithful. Clerics told cautionary tales about women in their sermons. For example, in a thirteenth-century sermon, Jacques de Vitry warned,

> they would rather take precedence, and they don't just despise their husbands, they lash out and beat them. . . . they always want to propose to put their will before their husbands' will. 'This is my will, and this is what I command: let will substitute for reason.' 'There was never a lawsuit which was not begun by a woman.' 'The marital bed is always a place of dispute and mutual bickering.'[13]

While these opinions would have been common currency, advocates of the goodness of women and for their education were also to be found. In *The Book of*

---

[12] C.E. Moreton, *The Townshends and Their World: Gentry, Law and Land in Norfolk, c. 1450–1551* (Oxford, 1992), p. 144.

[13] Jacques de Vitry, Sermon 66, in A. Blamires (ed.), *Woman Defamed and Woman Defended: An Anthology of Medieval Texts* (Oxford, 1992), p. 145.

the Courtier, which had wide currency in sixteenth-century England, Castiglione writes, 'And then, since words are idle and childish unless they are concerned with some subject of importance, the lady at Court as well as being able to recognize the rank of the person with whom she is talking should possess a knowledge of many subjects . . .'.[14] The reality in fifteenth-century England seems to mirror Castiglione's good opinion of women. One needs only to point to partnerships such as that of John and Margaret Paston. Naming a wife as an executor was quite common, which seems to indicate respect for women's abilities. Daughters and sisters were also named executors or given gifts of land to manage in their own right. Frequently, when property was given to sons, it was given jointly to them with their wives. And women were frequently given charge of the upbringing of minor male heirs as well as daughters when their husbands died. Their training – their education – was considered sufficient to enable them to fulfil these roles.

In her 1989 article 'Teach Her to Live under Obedience', Linda Pollock tells us that women in early modern England were theoretically expected to 'obey, evincing humility and deference',[15] while they 'proved in practice to be successful managers of estates, efficient organizers of popular protest, active participants in business, as well as being in the forefront of religious dissent'.[16] Women were to be competent and self-reliant, but compliant. Their training was to make them good helpmates to their future husbands.[17] Aristocratic women in fifteenth-century England would have been much like those in the seventeenth century in terms of self-reliance.

Women of various classes were integral to the education of aristocrats from birth – mothers, wet nurses, nursery mistresses and the other ladies of the household. The suitability of wet nurses and nursery attendants was considered

---

[14] Baldesar Castiglione, *The Book of the Courtier*, tr. G. Bull (Harmondsworth, 1967), p. 213.

[15] Linda Pollock, '"Teach Her to Live under Obedience": the Making of Women in the Upper Ranks of Early Modern England', *Continuity and Change*, 4 (2) (1989), 231.

[16] *Ibid.*, p. 231.

[17] *Ibid.*, p. 248.

extremely important as the nurse was thought to contribute something of her character with her milk and the shaping of character was considered an integral part of the educational process. The nurse was usually a free woman of artisanal status. For example, Richard II's nurse married the young king's tailor and the dry-nurse of Edward VI was married to a barber-surgeon. The nursery mistress was an aristocrat, especially in the case of the royal household. Some examples include the governess of Edward I's children, Marie de Valoynes; of Edward III's children, Elizabeth of St Omer and later Isabella de la Mote; of Henry VI's nursery, Elizabeth Ryman and Lady Alice Butler. These gentlewomen would be expected to teach noble children good manners and to take charge of the staff of the nursery. Margaret Hexstall, the governess of the duke of Buckingham's household, supervised a staff of seventeen. Her charges were the young heir and his sisters. Her duties included providing food for the children and the staff, deciding on the daily menus, and ensuring that the children had four or five dishes of meat and fish daily. Nicholas Orme states that specific educational duties were not indicated but might have been expected in the normal course of events.[18]

We know that many women were educated in the households of other families and others were instructed in nunneries.[19] The countess of Suffolk sent her daughter Philippa and her granddaughter Elizabeth to the priory at Bungay. Elizabeth was later sent to study at the abbey of Bruisyard.[20] Other alternatives seem to have been possible. C.L. Kingsford, the editor of the Stonor letters, posits that Jane Stonor, the daughter of an Oxfordshire gentleman, was educated abroad.[21] The family's strong connections with the wool staple in Calais make this very possible. However, Kingsford gives no indication whether Jane was educated in a religious house or in an aristocratic household.

---

[18] Nicholas Orme, 'The Education of a Courtier', in *Education and Society in Medieval and Renaissance England* (London, 1989), p. 161.

[19] E. Power, *Medieval People* (10th edn, London, 1963), p. 80.

[20] Jennifer C. Ward, *English Noblewomen in the Later Middle Ages* (London, 1992), p. 96.

[21] C.L. Kingsford (ed.), *The Stonor Letters and Papers, 1290–1483*, vol. I (London, Camden Society, Third Series, 1919), p. xxv.

A difficulty in discussing late medieval English education, especially for aristocratic women, is in the value judgements made about aristocratic education. For example, in her 1947 study, *Education in Fifteenth-Century England*, Clara P. McMahon starts her section on 'class education' with the statement, 'the systems of instruction were clear-cut and definite to the point of being narrowly utilitarian', and continues with her definition of chivalric education with the observation that 'Noble-born boys and girls were trained for social leadership and the management of the great estates to which they would eventually fall heir'. No one would argue these points. She goes on to say, however, that 'chivalric education came to be a shallow, meaningless system of training that wasted many precious years of the child's life. It should be remembered, too, that the refinements and traits of gentility inculcated in the well-born held true only for members of their own class. . . .'[22] We are now moving from the realm of description to value judgement. A more recent writer, Margaret King, also devalues the education of women who did not learn Greek and Latin. But her models of well-educated women are the learned women of Renaissance Italy and the English aristocracy seems to have found vernacular literature, both religious and secular, more congenial than the study of classical languages. Aristocrats were not persecuted for their preference for the vernacular, unlike the poorer classes, who could be accused of Lollardy for possessing vernacular texts.[23] Christine de Pizan, whom King discusses at length as a model of a learned woman, wrote most of her influential books and essays in French, even though she knew Latin.[24]

The standards of humanistic education have been used by modern historians to judge the aristocracy of late medieval England and find them wanting.

---

[22] C.P. McMahon, *Education in Fifteenth-Century England* (Baltimore, 1947), p. 123.

[23] Margaret Aston, 'Lollardy and Literacy', in *Lollards and Reformers: Images and Literacy in Late Medieval Religion* (London, 1984), pp. 208–9. The ordinances of St Albans (1426–7) prohibited 'books in the vulgar tongue' as indicating heretical beliefs because heresy could be caused by 'the possession and reading of books which were written in a vernacular tongue'.

[24] M.L. King, *Women of the Renaissance*, pp. 219–28. King defines the Renaissance broadly, covering the history of women from 1350 to 1650 and occasionally citing earlier examples.

Englishmen were going to Italy to imbibe humanist learning and humanists from the Continent were coming to England, looking for patrons. Pietro Carmeliano and Bernard André, for example, were appointed tutors to the royal household by Henry VII. André was also designated poet laureate and given 100s each year in honour of the new year.[25] But the education of most of the aristocracy did not follow the new humanistic curriculum. So equating humanism with 'real' education is a false equation. For example, Retha Warnicke, discussing women in Tudor England, states 'It is unreasonable to suggest that, because it had several learned women, Tudor society as a whole encouraged its gentlewomen to become well educated'.[26] Warnicke is making the assumption that early Tudor society defined 'well educated' in the same way as Sir Thomas More. While he had educated his daughters to read Latin and Greek, as well as having them taught logic, mathematics, and astronomy and how to write scholarly treatises, their contemporary, Katherine of Aragon, had a more 'limited' education, according to Warnicke. She and her sisters merely

> studied drawing, music, sewing, embroidery, weaving, spinning, baking, and handwriting. In addition, they learned to read in Latin the Christian poets, Prudentius and Juvencus; the Church Fathers, Ambrose, Augustine, Gregory, and Jerome; some of the ancient sages, particularly Seneca; and the law, both civil and canon.[27]

Katherine's education followed the lines suggested by the Spanish humanist Juan Luis Vives, who, as a member of Katherine's court, drew up a plan of education for the queen's daughter, Mary. Vives, concerned with inculcating a moral education, suggested a curriculum for the aristocratic woman.

---

[25] David Carlson, *English Humanist Books: Writers and Patrons, Manuscript and Print, 1475–1525* (Toronto, 1993), pp. 62–3.

[26] R.M. Warnicke, *Women of the English Renaissance and Reformation* (Westport, Conn., 1983), p. 4.

[27] *Ibid.*, p. 33.

When she shall be taught to read, let those books be taken in hand that may teach good manners. And when she shall learn to write, let not her example be void verses nor wanton or trifling songs but some sad sentences, prudent and chaste, taken out of holy scripture of the sayings of philosophers, which by often writing she may fasten better in her memory. . . .[28]

This was not an atypical education for a woman who was expected to run a household and an estate. As Warnicke admits, 'The wife's first duty, whether as a duchess or as a goodwoman, was housewifery, a task that was far more formidable than cleaning and dusting and keeping order'.[29] A classical education might be a nice accomplishment, but knowing about provisioning, attending to the illnesses of the household, protecting the estates in the absence of fathers, brothers and husbands, and dealing with legal matters were vital to the smooth running of estates. In general, their brothers were getting the same education – etiquette, music, reading, perhaps French. They would also ride. The difference was that the boys would also take part in such physical training as wrestling, archery, fencing and the like. Although it is true that by Jane Austen's time many of these necessary educational attributes had merely become empty accomplishments practised in the hope of attracting a husband, as she makes clear in *Pride and Prejudice* and other novels, these 'accomplishments' were still important components in the socialization of education of an upper-class Englishwoman in the fifteenth century. Embroidery, for example, 'was highly commended by moralists as a means of keeping ladies from idleness and, when it involved the making of vestments for clerics, contributing to the well-being of society'.[30] It was not seen as a vacuous, time-wasting occupation.

---

[28] Juan Luis Vives, 'A Cautious Curriculum for Noblewomen', in David Cressy (ed.), *Education in Tudor and Stuart England* (New York, 1975), p. 106.

[29] Warnicke, p. 6.

[30] Orme, 'Courtier', p. 173.

Religion was an important component of education. The Church directed that baptism, confirmation and learning prayers were necessary for everyone.[31] Giles of Rome wrote that children should be taught the articles of faith. Children were read religious stories and taken to services. On Palm Sunday, 1341, Edward III's daughters Isabella and Joan, aged nine and eight, listened to a sermon preached by a Dominican friar.[32]

Even before the Reformation, religion could be a spur to literacy. '[C]onstant repetition and reading aloud would have made the contents of scriptural texts familiar. Furthermore women may have received some formal instruction at home, as the households of great ladies had chaplains, books, and private chambers.'[33] The increase in literacy in the fifteenth century meant that religious instruction could move outside the church and into the household.[34] The demand for books also increased, especially religious texts, didactic literature and romances such as Bevis of Hampton and Guy of Warwick.[35] Cecily, duchess of York and mother of two kings, was renowned for her piety. She willed several books on religious subjects to her granddaughter, Bridgit, who had taken the veil. Commonplace books, like the one found in Brome, give examples of the religious literature favoured in households. They are collections of prayers, lists of the sacraments, the Ten Commandments, stories of saints and catechetical material such as 'The Catechism of Adrian Epotys'.[36]

Discussions of educated aristocratic women in fifteenth-century England tend to revolve around Margaret Beaufort and Cecily Neville, admittedly two extraordinary women. Cecily has been discussed above. Margaret Beaufort was the wealthiest woman in England while her son, Henry VII, was king. This was not merely a son's generosity to his mother. Margaret was a great heiress in her

---

[31] *Ibid.*, p. 155.

[32] *Ibid.*, p. 172.

[33] Clanchy, p. 189.

[34] Eamon Duffy, *The Stripping of the Altars: Traditional Religion in England, 1400–1580* (New Haven, 1992), p. 69.

[35] Duffy, p. 69.

[36] *Ibid.*, p. 74.

own right and she was granted the position of *femme sole* during Henry's reign, even though she was still married to Thomas, Lord Stanley. This was a testament to her ability. Henry trusted Margaret's judgement. 'The one person [in the king's family] whose influence was paramount was the King's own mother, Margaret Beaufort. From her household a constant stream of people emerged to find employment in Henry's household, council, and service.'[37] Margaret Beaufort was an excellent judge of character and her household was an educational training ground for future servants of her son, Henry VII.[38]

Although few women could be mothers of kings, other examples of educated aristocratic women can be found, for example, Anne Harling of East Harling, Norfolk. The only child of Sir Robert Harling and Anne Gonville, an heiress, Anne Harling was a benefactress to her community through generous bequests to various churches and she was also very interested in education. She had been the ward of Sir John Fastolf, and was married first to Sir William Chamberlain, then to Sir Robert Wingfield and finally to Lord Scrope of Bolton.[39] She was well educated, had wealth and influence, was literate and learned, and was noted for her piety. Anne Harling had her own books and could read in English and French. She owned and managed manors and estates in various parts of England, wielded political influence, made bequests to institutions that promoted education and supported both teachers and students.[40]

Other extraordinary, and extraordinarily influential, women included Margaret, duchess of Burgundy, Queen Elizabeth Woodville, Alice Chaucer, Alice de Bryene and Elizabeth Talbot. They had an interest in education, as did Elizabeth of York, wife of Henry VII. Her privy purse accounts show payment of 6*d* in March 1503 for a book as a gift for Edward Pallett, the son of Lady Jane Bangham. Edward was

---

[37] Margaret Condon, 'Ruling Elites in the Reign of Henry VII', in Charles Ross (ed.), *Patronage, Pedigree and Power in Later Medieval England* (Gloucester, 1979), p. 114.

[38] Condon, 'Ruling Elites', p. 114.

[39] G. McMurray Gibson, *The Theater of Devotion: East Anglian Drama and Society in the Late Middle Ages* (Chicago, 1989), p. 96.

[40] *Ibid.*, pp. 96–106.

brought up at the queen's expense.[41] Another boy brought up at the queen's expense was John Pertriche. In March 1503, the record shows payments of 20*d* for 'his lernyng' and 20*d* for a primer and psalter.[42] Their interests and positions made all these women extraordinary among the English population as a whole. And yet, by the standards of historians like McMahon, King and Warnicke, Anne Harling, Margaret Beaufort, Cecily Neville and the other women mentioned above were not well educated. Certainly they had never been to school. They did not know any Greek, and little or no Latin. But this is too narrow a definition. They were very well educated by the standards of their time. While classical languages were not widely studied in the upper classes by either sex, French was taught to many aristocratic women. French was no longer the language of common conversation in England, and Chaucer belittled the prioress's knowledge, saying

> And Frenssh she spak ful faire and fetisly,
> After the scole of Stratford atte Bowe,
> For Frenssh of Parys was to hire unknowe.[43]

However, the aristocracy still made an effort to learn acceptable French, to read French books and to correspond in French. The Lanthony Priory letter book from 1424 contains letters in French from the countess of Stafford.[44] Knowing French was considered a mark of aristocratic status.[45] Alexander Barclay (1475?–1552) wrote, '[French] hath ben so moche set by in England that who hath ben ignorant in the same language hath not ben reputed to be of gentyll blode'.[46]

---

[41] N.H. Nicolas (ed.), *Privy Purse Expenses of Elizabeth of York: Wardrobe Accounts of Edward the Fourth. With a Memoir of Elizabeth of York, and Notes* (London, 1830), p. 98.

[42] *Ibid.*, p. 105.

[43] Geoffrey Chaucer, 'General Prologue', *The Canterbury Tales*, ll. 124–6, ed. F.N. Robinson (Boston, 1957), p. 18.

[44] D. Kibbee, *For to Speke Frenche Trewly. The French Language in England, 1000–1600: Its Status, Description and Instruction* (Amsterdam, 1991), p. 72.

[45] *Ibid.*, p. 101.

[46] *Idem*, p. 101.

In the Plumpton correspondence of the same period we find one grandfather writing to another, 'Your [grand]daughter and mine speaketh prettily and French and hath neat hand, and learned her psalter'; and she was only three.[47] Margaret Beaufort was known for her translations from French, especially the fourth book of the *Imitation of Christ* by Thomas à Kempis, which was published by Richard Pynson in 1504.[48] However, while she was more than proficient in French, Margaret's command of Latin only allowed her to read the headings in her service books.[49]

What was the point of the education that McMahon judges so severely? Court and household life was expected to reflect the status of the individual. The greatest peers were expected to dress extravagantly, give wonderful gifts, use gilded dishes and entertain lavishly. But one of the most important indicators of high social standing was having the leisure time to engage in activities such as hunting for pleasure, dancing, gambling and performing in tournaments. Courteous behaviour was important, as was the ability to eat properly. Defining the nature of French noble education in the sixteenth century, Mark Motley wrote, 'It is difficult to exaggerate the importance of behavior at table in a child's education, for eating remained the great public event of the household day . . .'.[50] Learning proper table manners was nothing new. A century or two earlier, Chaucer's Prioress, while not proficient in French, certainly knew how to eat properly:

> At mete wel ytaught was she with alle:
> She leet no moresel from hir lippes falle,
> Ne wette hir fyngres in hir sauce depe;
> Wel koude she carie a morsel and wel kepe
> That no drope ne fille upon hire brest.
> In curteisie was set ful muchel hir lest.[51]

---

[47] Power, p. 85. Nicholas Orme puts her age at four, *From Childhood to Chivalry*, p. 127.

[48] M.K. Jones, and M.G. Underwood, *The King's Mother: Lady Margaret Beaufort, Countess of Richmond and Derby* (Cambridge, 1992), p. 184.

[49] *Ibid.*, p. 184.

[50] M. Motley, *Becoming a French Aristocrat: The Education of the Court Nobility, 1580–1715* (Princeton, 1990), p. 17.

[51] Chaucer, 'General Prologue', ll. 127–32 (p. 18).

In 'The Babees Book', written about 1475, aristocratic English children were told:

> Oute ouere youre dysshe your heede yee nat hynge,
> And withe fulle mouthe drynkein no wyse;
> Youre nose, your teethe, your naylles, from pykynge,
> Kepe at your mete, for sotechis wyse,
> Eke or ye take in youre mouthe, you avyse,
> So mekyl mete but that yee rihte welle mow
> Answere, and speke, whenne men speke to yow.[52]

The education in a household such as that of Margaret Beaufort was a sought-after form of favour. While the famous Venetian visitor of about 1500 might profess to be shocked that the English sent their children to other households to be educated,[53] this method not only created a tie between households but brought children into contact with larger society. Kate Mertes describes the medieval noble household as 'a collection of servants, friends and other retainers, around a noble and possibly his immediate family, all of whom lived together unde[r] the same roof(s) as a single community'.[54] Children were taught how to serve at table, how to enter a room, and how to behave when a social superior demanded attention. The Pastons' letters are filled with discussions about placing children, especially daughters, in various households. Alice de Bryene had boys who were not her children living in her household, serving as pages. Possibly some of them were from gentry families in the neighbourhood who were gaining an education through service.[55] The serving members of the household –

[52] 'The Babees Book', in F.J. Furnivall (ed.), *Early English Meals and Manners* (London, 1868), p. 255.

[53] C.A. Sneyd (ed.), *A Relation or Rather a True Account, of the Island of England; with Sundry Particulars of the Customs of These People, and of the Royal Revenues under King Henry the Seventh about the Year 1500* (London, Camden Society, 1847), p. 20.

[54] Kate Mertes, *The English Noble Household, 1250–1600* (Oxford, 1988), p. 5.

[55] E. Acheson, *A Gentry Community: Leicestershire in the Fifteenth Century, c. 1422–c. 1485* (Cambridge, 1992), p. 177.

frequently younger sons and daughters – were usually making family connections, 'serving as henchmen, pages and companions to the lady while completing their education in a grand establishment',[56] or they might be family heirs who were being 'finished' in a suitable environment and 'also achieved early connections for themselves and their families through their positions'.[57] The willingness to take children into a noble household was part of the medieval idea of hospitality. Felicity Heal, discussing hospitality in early modern England, states, 'Honour and reputation attached to good lordship, generosity, and the appearance of an open household: these were sentiments generally expressed in early modern English culture'.[58] Of course, these sentiments were also powerful in motivating social conduct in late medieval England.

The royal household was unsurpassed for the schooling that it provided, not only for the king's children but for the other children at court.[59] The education provided at court consisted of two parts: *noriture* and *lettrure*. *Noriture* consisted of etiquette, athletics, dancing, music, the composition of poetry and other artistic and physical achievements. *Lettrure* stressed reading and writing in French, English and Latin, the study of practical rather than imaginative literature, and fostered the study of grammar and history. History was stressed because it was considered to be entertaining, honoured ancestors and provided practical examples of good and bad conduct.[60]

Schooling might be a final touch in male education in the fifteenth century. For upper-class men not dedicated to the Church, the universities and the Inns of Court were seen as lending polish for a life dominated by courtly expectations and legal battles. Women, of course, were not allowed to attend institutions of higher education.

[56] Mertes, *Noble Household*, p. 60.

[57] *Idem*, p. 60.

[58] F. Heal, *Hospitality and Society in Early Modern England* (Cambridge, 1990), p. 13.

[59] Sneyd (ed.), *Relation*, p. 20.

[60] R. Firth Green, *Poets and Princepleasers: Literature and the English Court in the Late Middle Ages* (Toronto, 1980), p. 73.

In an age when aristocratic education did not take place in school and documentation is scarce, we can only speculate on the processes by which upper-class women were educated. However, the patronage of writers, teachers, schools and scholars is one possible way to assess women's interest in education. Linda Pollock characterizes patronage as a 'contract' between the patron and the client that was cemented by the idea of honour.[61] The vertical giving of patronage gave prestige to the giver as well as to the recipient. For the client, patronage could mean the garnering of lands, money and titles. For the patron, patronage was attractive because the promotion of clients enhanced the standing and reputation of the patron. Elizabeth of York might have patronized Edward Pallett and John Pertriche out of a genuine sense of charity and piety. However, such patronage also enhanced her reputation for generosity. The provision of political patronage frequently garnered gifts and money for the patron as inducements to provide offices, appointments or access to another influential person. With literary patronage, a writer could glorify the patron in a public and lasting way. Authors hoped for an outright gift of money or more valuable forms of patronage such as offices. These offices might be religious preferments, appointments as tutors or secretaries, university fellowships and masterships in schools. Prominent men wished to be patrons because conspicuous consumption was a mark of nobility, the propaganda produced by the patronized was beneficial to the patron and the patronage could be used to establish a position within their class.[62] Aristocratic women in fifteenth-century England would have been as interested in, and were as likely to have been patrons of, education as men were. An influential patron like Margaret, duchess of Burgundy could not only support Caxton but persuade her brother Edward IV to patronize him as well.

---

[61] L. Pollock, 'Younger Sons in Tudor and Stuart England', *History Today*, 39 (June 1989), 29: 'Patron-client alliances were types of contract in which prestige flowed to the patron and wealth and resources to the client.'

[62] Some studies of patronage that seem especially useful are R. Firth Green, *Poets and Princepleasers*, H.S. Bennett's classic *English Books and Readers, 1475–1557*, 2nd edn (Cambridge, 1969, 1989), Alistair Fox's *Politics and Literature in the Reigns of Henry VII and Henry VIII* (Oxford, 1989).

Noblewomen were well-known patrons of colleges. In 1448 Margaret of Anjou founded Queens' College, Cambridge, and the college was later supported by Elizabeth Woodville and Anne Neville. Margaret Beaufort not only provided a professorship but she also induced her ward, the duke of Buckingham, to donate 31 acres of land for its upkeep.[63]

Women patrons were frequently connected to each other. For example, Joan Beaufort was well known as a patroness. Her daughters Cecily and Anne Neville were also known as patrons of various authors. Sisters Eleanor and Mary Bohun were also noted patrons and Eleanor is especially known for having commissioned the Edinburgh Psalter. Eleanor's daughter Anne, countess of Stafford, patronized John Lydgate's *Invocation to St Anne*, and Anne's daughter Anne, wife of the earl of March, patronized Lydgate's *Legend of St Margaret*.[64]

Margaret, duchess of Burgundy was not the only well-known patroness of Caxton. *The Book of the Knight of the Tower* was a fourteenth-century manual describing, through various stories and homilies, appropriate female behaviour that Geoffrey la Tour Landry, a French nobleman, wrote for the instruction of his own daughters. In his English translation of this treatise, Caxton says of another of his patronesses, that the

> boke is comen to my handes by the request & desyre of a noble lady which hath brouȝt forth many noble & fayr douȝters which ben vertuously nourisshed & lerned/ And for very ziele & loue that she hath alway had to her fayr children & yet hath for to haue more knouleche in vertue to thende that they may alwey perseuere in the same hath desired & required me to translate & reduece this said book out of frenssh in to our vulgar englisshe/ to thende that it may the better be vnderstonde of al such as shal rede or here it/

---

[63] Darlene Tempelton, *Woman in Yorkist England* (Mesquite, Tex., 1983), p. 17.

[64] Carol Meale, '". . . alle the bokes that I haue of latyn, englisch, and frensch": laywomen and their books in late medieval England', in C. Meale (ed.), *Women and Literature in Britain, 1150–1500* (Cambridge, 1993), p. 130.

wherfor atte contemplacion of her good grace after the lytel connyng that god hath sent me/ I haue endeuoyryd me to obeye her noble desyre & request especial for ladyes & gentilsymen dou3ters to lordes & gentilmen/ For whiche book al the gentilwymen now lyuyng & herafter to come or shal be arn bounde to gyue laude praysying & thanynges to the auctor of this book & also to the lady that caused me to translate it . . .[65]

Nicholas Orme has speculated that this noble patroness might have been Queen Elizabeth Woodville, wife of Edward IV.[66]

Another form of patronage was the supporting of scholars at schools. Margaret Beaufort's interest in educating her servants (of all classes) can be seen in the apprenticeships she secured for some and the maintenance for scholars that she provided. 'Scholars from Lady Margaret's chapel were supported at Eton, the London Charterhouse, Oxford and Cambridge.'[67] Another woman with an interest in education was Dame Joan Chamberlain of York, wife of William Chamberlain, esquire.[68] In her will of 1502, Dame Joan directed that her property in Hundgate be sold 'and the money for the said to be disposid for the wele of my saule; that is to say to the exhibicion of pure chylder apte to lerne at scoles . . .'.[69]

The foundation of chantries to say masses for the souls of the dead was thought to be an avenue out of purgatory. It was also a form of educational patronage. For example, in 1486, John Hosyer of Ludlow left funds for the foundation of an almshouse and chantry. Not only did he provide for a priest who would say mass for the denizens of the almshouses and pray for the souls of Hosyer and his wife, Alice, but 'six of the best voiced singing children' were to be

[65] Geoffrey la Tour Landry, *The Book of the Knight of the Tower*, tr. by William Caxton and ed. by M.Y. Offord (London, 1971), p. 3.

[66] Orme, *From Childhood to Chivalry*, p. 108.

[67] Jones and Underwood, p. 167.

[68] This was a different William Chamberlain to the one married to Anne Harling.

[69] *Testamenta Eboracensia. A Selection of Wills from the Registry at York*, vol. IV (Durham, 1869), p. 202.

employed as well.[70] When the children needed to be replaced, 'whenever the voice or voices of any of the said six children shall happen to change or fail, or else any of the said six children be of evil condition, then and so often the said warden and feoffees shall remove the same child or children, and put other well-voiced, willing to learn song, in his or their place or places . . .'.[71] Obviously the chantry was also to function as a song school.

Testamentary bequests of books is another way in which we might discover something about the education of women. Of course, wills only reflect a small and possibly skewed portion of the female population since many wills do not survive and most wills were made by single women and widows. In late medieval England, most married women did not make wills because their movable property was under the control of their husbands.[72] The wills were not complete inventories of moveable goods and probably did not include all the books owned by the testator, only those that seemed particularly valuable.[73] Frequently these books, especially psalters, primers, and the like, had intrinsic value as objects, being decorated with gold and silver.[74] In 1427, in the will of Elizabeth, Lady Fitzhugh, she gives

[M]y son Rob't a sauter couered with' rede velvet and my doghter Marjory a primer cou'ed in Rede and my doghter Darcy a sauter cou'ed in blew & my doghter Malde Eure a prim' cou'ed in blew . . . And yong Elyzabeth ffitzhugh my goddaughter a book cou'ed in grene with praiers.[75]

[70] R.N. Swanson, *Catholic England: Faith, Religion and Observance before the Reformation* (Manchester, 1993), pp. 236–7.

[71] *Ibid.*, p. 237.

[72] Meale, p. 130; Richard Helmholtz, 'Married Women's Wills in Later Medieval England', in Walker (ed.), *Wife and Widow*, pp. 165–83.

[73] Meale, p. 130.

[74] *Idem.*

[75] *Wills and Inventories Illustrative of the History, Manners, Language, Statistics etc. of the Northern Counties of England, from the Eleventh Century Downwards*, Part I (London, Publications of the Surtees Society, vol. 2, 1835), pp. 74–5.

While other items of property are mentioned, such as jewelry and items of clothing, and instructions are given for masses and the settling of debts, obviously these books – all religious in nature – were considered to be important property that was to be passed on to other members of the Fitzhugh family. Anne Harling's will includes gifts such as 'To my lady my lorde moder, myn embrowdered Sawter'.[76] Perhaps more interesting is her gift to her godson, the duke of Suffolk. Among other bequests, Anne gave him 'a Premer whiche kynge Edward gauffe me'.[77] The importance of the gift to the duke might be the connection with the previous owner. Edward IV may have given her the book because of her pious reputation and her interest in books. Anne Harling had other books which she considered valuable and were mentioned in her will. Her nephew Edward received 'a Frenche boke'.[78] Dame Jane Blakeney received 'my white booke of Prayers'.[79] Her god-daughter, Anne Fitzwater, received 'a Premer clasped w^t silver and gylte, for a remembraunce, to pray for me'.[80] A less-exalted lady, Dame Margery Salvin of York, wife of Sir John Salvin, left her brother, Richard Danby, her 'boke of Bocas'[81] at her death in 1496. Books were considered valuable commodities, worth giving and receiving, and well worth protection. In February 1503, the privy purse accounts for Elizabeth of York record a payment to William Trende of 18s to reimburse him 'for money by him layed out for the making of a chest and almorys in the Quenes Counsaille Chambre for to put in the bokes'.[82]

Whether the testator or the legatees could read the books is not really important. They were doubtless part of a community in which some members could read. In addition, these books could act as an aide-mémoire in the daily practice of religion. Eric Acheson, in his study of the Leicestershire gentry in the

---

[76] *Testamenta Eboracensia*, vol. IV, 152.

[77] *Idem.*

[78] *Idem.*

[79] *Idem.*

[80] *Ibid.*, p. 153.

[81] *Ibid.*, p. 116.

[82] *Privy Purse Expenses of Elizabeth of York*, p. 96.

fifteenth century, points out that a book received as a bequest might not have had much value for its new owner.[83] While this may be true, the book certainly had some importance to the testator. Religious books could serve a commemorative function, reminding the recipient of the giver each time it was used.[84] These books may therefore be one small measure of an interest in education in its broadest sense.

Looking at women book owners is a fruitful way of measuring an interest in literate culture. Anne Beauchamp, the wife of Richard Neville, earl of Warwick, gave her *Book of Hours*, an elaborately illustrated work said to have been commissioned for her by her father, to her daughter Anne, the wife of Richard III. Margaret Beaufort had an impressive library. Edward IV willed several books to his wife, Elizabeth Woodville, including St Augustine's *City of God*; she also owned *The Romance of the Holy Grail*, and the *Morte d'Arthur*. Margaret of Anjou, the wife of Henry VI, read Boccaccio and owned romances about Alexander the Great, Charlemagne, Ogier the Dane and Guy of Warwick. Her book collection also included *Le Livre de Fais Darmes et de Chevalries* by Christine de Pizan and *Le Ordre de Gartier*.[85] Jo Ann Hoeppner Moran found in her study of education in Yorkshire that women's wills were more likely to include books among bequests than were men's wills.[86] This may be because women were more likely to own moveables than land. While the mere ownership of books does not prove that these ladies could read – they could, after all, have had a servant or relative read to them – it does show that they were interested in and participated in literate society.

Although higher education was not an option for aristocratic women, their household education was very much like that of men. If Nicholas Orme is correct in his assumption that there was a lack of a specific educational consciousness

---

[83] Acheson, *A Gentry Community*, p. 187.

[84] Meale, p. 131.

[85] Tempelton, p. 16.

[86] J.A. Hoeppner Moran, *The Growth of English Schooling, 1348–1548: Learning, Literacy, and Laicization in Pre-Reformation York Diocese* (Princeton, 1985), p. 152.

with regard to training upper-class children, this factor may have worked to women's advantage.[87] Upper-class women were members of literate society whether or not they could participate directly, despite the advice of Philippe de Novare in *Les quatre âges d'homme*: 'Teach women neither letters nor writing'.[88] With their brothers, aristocratic women were educated with the position they would hold in mind. Like their fathers, brothers and husbands, they managed estates, read religious and secular literature, participated in courtly pastimes, pursued legal cases and oversaw the education of their own children as well as the children of other families. The practical, rather than the theoretical, basis that seems to have been prominent in late medieval thinking about education meant that the training which upper-class women received had to equip them to meet the obligations that society would impose on them. In addition, the importance of religion in late medieval society and the need for religious instruction were both an impetus to, and a major component of, women's education.

[87] Orme, 'Education of the Courtier', p. 157.

[88] D. Régnier-Bohler, 'Literary and Mystical Voices', in C. Klapisch-Zuber (ed.), *A History of Women*, vol. 2, *Silences of the Middle Ages* (Cambridge, 1992), p. 442.

SELECT BIBLIOGRAPHY

Aberth, John. *Criminal Churchmen in the Age of Edward III: The Case of Bishop Thomas de Lisle*, University Park, Penn., 1996

Acheson, E. *A Gentry Community: Leicestershire in the Fifteenth Century, c. 1422–c.1485*, Cambridge, 1992

Allmand, C.T. *Henry V*, London, 1992

Anglo, Sydney. 'The British History in Early Tudor Propaganda', *Bulletin of the John Rylands Library* 44 (1961)

Archer, R.E. and Walker, S. (eds). *Rulers and Ruled in Late Medieval England*, London, 1995

Armstrong, C.A.J. *England, France and Burgundy in the Fifteenth Century*, London, 1983

Aston, M. *Lollards and Reformers: Images and Literacy in Late Medieval Religion*, London, 1984

Aston, M. and Richmond, C. *Lollardy and the Gentry in the Later Middle Ages*, Stroud, 1997

Attreed, L.C. 'A New Source for Perkin Warbeck's Invasion of 1497', *Medieval Studies* XLVIII (1986)

Axon, William E.A. 'A Manchester Will of the Fifteenth Century', *Echoes of Old Lancashire*, 1899

Aylmer, G.E. 'From Office-Holding to Civil Service: The Genesis of Modern Bureaucracy', *Transactions of the Royal Historical Society*, 5th series, XXX (1980)

Bain, Joseph (ed.). *Calendar of Documents relating to Scotland*, 4 vols, Edinburgh, 1881–8

Baker, J.H. *An Introduction to English Legal History*, 3rd edition, London, 1990

Baker, J.H. (ed.). *Legal Records and the Historian*, London, 1978

Barron, C.M. 'London and the Crown, 1451–61', in Highfield and Jeffs (eds), *The Crown and Local Communities in England and France in the Fifteenth Century*, Gloucester, 1981

Bennett, H.S. *English Books and Readers, 1475–1557*, Cambridge, 1969

Benson, Pamela J. *The Invention of the Renaissance Woman: The Challenge of Female Independence in the Literature and Thought of Italy and England*, University Park, Penn., 1992

Bernard, G. (ed.). *The Tudor Nobility*, Manchester, 1992

Blamires, A. (ed.). *Woman Defamed and Woman Defended: An Anthology of Medieval Texts*, Oxford, 1992

Blatcher, M. *The Court of King's Bench, 1450–1550*, London, 1978

Bonney, R. (ed.). *Economic Systems and State Finance*, Oxford, 1995

Britnell, R.H. 'The Pastons and their Norfolk', *Agricultural History Review* 36 (1988)

Brodie, D.M. (ed.). *The Tree of the Commonwealth: A Treatise Written by Edmund Dudley*, Cambridge, 1948

Brown, A.L. 'The Privy Seal Clerks in the Early Fifteenth Century', in D.A. Bullough and R.A. Storey (eds), *The Study of Medieval Records: Essays in Honour of Kathleen Major*, Oxford, 1971

Bullough, D.A. and Storey, R.A. (eds). *The Study of Medieval Records: Essays in Honour of Kathleen Major*, Oxford, 1971

Campbell, John, Lord. *The Lives of the Lord Chancellors and Keepers of the Great Seal of England*, 8 vols, London, 1846–69

Carlson, David. *English Humanist Books: Writers and Patrons, Manuscript and Print, 1475–1525*, Toronto, 1993

Castiglione, Baldesar. *The Book of the Courtier*, trans. G. Bull, Harmondsworth, 1967

Cheney, C.R. (ed.). *Handbook of Dates for Students of English History*, London, 1978

Chrimes, S.B. *Introduction to the Administrative History of Medieval England*, Oxford, 1952

Chrimes, S.B., Ross, C.D., and Griffiths, R.A. (eds). *Fifteenth-Century England*, 2nd edition, Stroud, 1995

Christine de Pizan. *A Medieval Woman's Mirror of Honor: The Treasure of the City of Ladies*, trans. C.C. Willard, ed. M.P. Cosman, New York, 1989

Clanchy, M.T. *From Memory to Written Record. England, 1066–1307*, London, 1979

Clayton, D.J. *The Administration of the County Palatine of Chester, 1442–85*, The Chetham Society, Manchester, 1990

Cockburn, J.S. *A History of the English Assizes, 1558–1714*, Cambridge, 1972

——. *Introduction to the Calendar of Assize Records, Home Circuit Indictments, Elizabeth I and James I*, London, 1985

Cockburn, J.S. and Green, T.A. (eds). *Twelve Good Men and True: the Criminal Trial Jury in England, 1200–1800*, Princeton, N.J., 1988

Condon, M.M. 'From Caitiff and Willain to Pater Patriae: Reynold Bray and the Profits of Office', in M.A. Hicks (ed.), *Profit, Piety, and the Professions in Later Medieval England*, Gloucester, 1990

——. 'Ruling Elites in the Reign of Henry VII', in Charles Ross, *Patronage, Pedigree and Power in Later Medieval England*, Gloucester, 1979

Cook, G.H. *Mediaeval Chantries and Chantry Chapels*, London, 1963

Cosgrove, A. (ed.). *A New History of Ireland*, volume II, Oxford, 1987

Coward, B. *The Stanleys, Lords Stanley and Earls of Derby, 1385–1672*, Manchester, 1983

Cressy, David (ed.). *Education in Tudor and Stuart England*, New York, 1975

Davies, C.S.L. 'Richard III, Henry VII and the Island of Jersey', *The Ricardian* IX, no. 119 (1992)

Davis, N. (ed.). *Paston Letters and Papers of the Fifteenth Century*, 2 vols, Oxford, 1971–6

Denholm-Young, N. *Seignorial Administration in England*, Oxford, 1937

Devon, F. (ed.). *Issues of the Exchequer, Henry III–Henry VI*, London, 1837

Dockray, K. 'The Origins of the Wars of the Roses', in A.J. Pollard (ed.), *The Wars of the Roses*, London, 1995

Duffy, Eamon. *The Stripping of the Altars. Traditional Religion in England, 1400–1580*, London, 1992

Dunham, jr, W.H. *The English Government at Work*, Cambridge, Mass., 1940

Dunn, D. (ed.). *Courts, Counties and the Capital in the Later Middle Ages*, Stroud, 1996

Eagleston, A.J. *The Channel Islands under Tudor Government, 1485–1642*, Cambridge, 1949

Eales, R. and Sullivan, D. (eds). *The Political Context of Law*, London, 1987

Elton, G.R. 'A Revolution in Tudor History', *Past and Present* XXXII (1965)

——. 'Henry VII: Rapacity and Remorse', *Historical Journal* I (1958)

——. 'Henry VII: a Restatement', *Historical Journal* IV (1961)

——. 'The Tudor Revolutions: a Reply', *Past and Present* XXIX (1964)

——. *The Tudor Revolution in Government: Administrative Changes in the Reign of Henry VIII*, Cambridge, 1953

Emden, A.B. *A Biographical Register of the University of Cambridge to 1500*, Cambridge, 1963

——. *A Biographical Register of the University of Oxford to AD 1500*, 3 vols, Oxford, 1957–9

Evans, H.T. *Wales and the Wars of the Roses*, 2nd edition, Stroud, 1995

Fianu, Kouky and Guth, DeLloyd J. *Ecrit et Pouvoir dans le Chancelleries Medievales: Espace Français, Espace Anglais*, Louvain-La-Neuve, 1997

Firth Green, R. *Poets and Princepleasers: Literature and the English Court in the Late Middle Ages*, Toronto, 1980

Fleming, P.W. 'Charity, Faith and the Gentry of Kent', in A.J. Pollard (ed.), *Property and Politics: Essays in Later Medieval English History*, Gloucester, 1984

Fortescue, J. *The Governance of England*, ed. C. Plummer, London, 1885

Foss, E. *Biographical Dictionary of the Judges of England*, London, 1870

Foss, P.J. *The Field of Redemore: The Battle of Bosworth, 1485*, Leeds, 1990

Fox, Alistair. *Politics and Literature in the Reigns of Henry VII and Henry VIII*, Oxford, 1989

Fryde, E.B., Greenway, D.E., Porter, S., and Roy, I. (eds). *Handbook of British Chronology*, London, 1986

Furnivall, F.J. (ed.). *Early English Meals and Manners*, London, 1868

Gairdner, J. (ed.). *The Paston Letters*, 6 vols, London, 1904

Gerould, Gordon Hall. 'A Text of Merlin's Prophecies', *Speculum* XXIII (1948)

Gibson, G. McMurray, *The Theater of Devotion: East Anglian Drama and Society in the Late Middle Ages*, Chicago, 1989

Goodman, A.E. 'The Anglo-Scottish Marches in the Fifteenth Century', in R.A. Mason (ed.), *Scotland and England, 1286–1815*, Edinburgh, 1987

——. *The Wars of the Roses: Military Activity and English Society, 1452–97*, London, 1981

Gransden, Antonia. *Historical Writing in England II*. c. *1307 to the Early Sixteenth Century*, London, 1982

Griffiths, R.A. 'Local Rivalries and National Politics: the Percies, the Nevilles and the Duke of Exeter, 1452–1454', *Speculum* XLIII (1968)

——. 'Public and Private Bureaucracies in England and Wales in the Fifteenth Century', *Transactions of the Royal Historical Society*, 5th series XXX (1980)

——. 'Wales and the Marches', in S.B. Chrimes, C.D. Ross and R.A. Griffiths, *Fifteenth-Century England*, 2nd edition, Stroud, 1995

——. *King and Country: England and Wales in the Fifteenth Century*, London, 1991

——. *Sir Rhys ap Thomas and His Family: A Study in the Wars of the Roses and Early Tudor Politics*, Cardiff, 1993

——. *The Reign of King Henry VI*, London, 1981

Griffiths, R.A. and Sherborne, J. (eds). *Kings and Nobles in the Later Middle Ages: A Tribute to Charles Ross*, Gloucester, 1986

Griffiths, R.A. (ed.). *Patronage, the Crown and the Provinces in Later Medieval England*, Gloucester, 1981

Gurr, A. (ed.). *King Henry V*, Cambridge, 1992

Guth, DeLloyd J. 'Enforcing Late Medieval Law: Patterns in Litigation during Henry VII's Reign', in J.H. Baker (ed.), *Legal Records and the Historian*, London, 1978

——. 'Fifteenth-Century England: Recent Scholarship and Future Directions', *British Studies Monitor* VII (1976)

——. 'Sir Reginald [*sic*] Bray: "Not He That Made the Smoke"', *Report of the Society of the Friends of St George's and the Descendants of the Knights of the Garter*, ed. M.H. Bond, 1970–1

——. *Late-medieval England, 1377–1485*, Cambridge, 1976

Guy, J.A. *Tudor England*, Oxford, 1988

Hallissy, Margaret. *Clean Maids, True Wives, Steadfast Widows, Chaucer's Women and Medieval Codes of Conduct*, Westport, Conn., 1993

Hammond, P.W. *The Battles of Barnet and Tewkesbury*, Gloucester, 1990

Hammond, P.W. (ed.). *Richard III: Loyalty, Lordship and Law*, London, 1986

Hanham, A. *Richard III and His Early Historians, 1483–1535*, Oxford, 1975

Harriss, G.L. 'The Struggle for Calais: an Aspect of the Rivalry between Lancaster and York', *English Historical Review* LXXV (1960)

Harvey, J.H. (ed.). *William Worcestre: Itineraries*, Oxford, 1969

Hastings, M. *The Court of Common Pleas in Fifteenth-Century England*, Ithaca, N.Y., 1947

Heal, F. *Hospitality and Society in Early Modern England*, Cambridge, 1990

Herbert, A. 'Herefordshire, 1413–61: Some Aspects of Society and Public Order', in R.A. Griffiths, *The Reign of King Henry VI*, London, 1981

Hicks, M.A. 'The Last Days of Elizabeth, Countess of Oxford', *English Historical Review* 103 (1988).

Hicks, M.A. (ed.). *Profit, Piety, and the Professions in Later Medieval England*, Gloucester, 1990

Highfield, J.R.L. and Jeffs, R.M. (eds). *The Crown and Local Communities in England and France in the Fifteenth Century*, Gloucester, 1981

Hoeppner Moran, J.A. *The Growth of English Schooling, 348–1548: Learning, Literacy, and Laicization in Pre-Reformation York Diocese*, Princeton, 1985

Hope, Andrew. 'The Lady and the Bailiff: Lollardy among the Gentry in Yorkist and Early Tudor England', in M. Aston and C. Richmond, *Lollardy and Gentry in the Later Middle Ages*, Stroud, 1997

Horrox, R. *Richard III: A Study of Service*, Cambridge, 1989

Houlbrooke, R.A. *The English Family, 1450–1700*, London, 1984

Hull, Suzanne W. *Chaste, Silent & Obedient: English Books for Women, 1475–1640*, San Marino, Calif., 1982

——. *Women According to Men: The World of Tudor-Stuart Women*, Walnut Creek, Calif., 1996

Isenmann, E. 'Medieval and Renaissance Theories of State Finance', in R. Bonney (ed.), *Economic Systems and State Finance*, Oxford, 1995

Ives, E.W. *The Common Lawyers of Pre-Reformation England. Thomas Kebell: A Case Study*, Cambridge, 1983

Johnson, P.A. *Duke Richard of York, 1411–1460*, Oxford, 1988

Jones, M.K. and Underwood, M.G. *The King's Mother: Lady Margaret Beaufort, Countess of Richmond and Derby*, Cambridge, 1992

Kibbee, D. *For to Speke Frenche Trweley. The French Language in England, 1000–1600: Its Status, Description and Instruction*, Amsterdam, 1991

Kingsford, C.L. (ed.). *The Stonor Letters and Papers*, 2 vols, London, 1919–21

Kitchin, G.W. (ed.). *The Records of the Northern Convocation*, Durham, 1907

Klapishch Zuber, C. (ed.). *A History of Women*, vol. 2, *Silences of the Middle Ages*, Cambridge, 1992

la Tour Landry, Geoffrey. *The Book of the Knight of the Tower*, trans. William Caxton, ed. M.Y. Offord, London, 1971

Lander, J.R. 'Council, Administration and Councillors, 1461 to 1485', *Bulletin of the Institute of Historical Research* 32 (1959)

——. *Crown and Nobility, 1450–1509*, London, 1976

——. *Government and Community: England, 1450–1509*, London, 1980

Latham, R.E. *Revised Medieval Latin Word-List*, London, 1965

Luckett, D. 'Crown Office and Licensed Retinues in the Reign of Henry VII', in R.E. Archer and S. Walker (eds), *Rulers and Ruled in Late Medieval England*, London, 1995

Macdougall, N. *James III*, Edinburgh, 1982

——. *James IV*, Edinburgh, 1989

Macfarlane, A. *Marriage and Love in England: Modes of Reproduction, 1300–1800*, Oxford, 1986

McMahon, C.P. *Education in Fifteenth-Century England*, Baltimore, 1947

Mason, R.A. (ed.). *Scotland and England, 1286–1815*, Edinburgh, 1987

Matthew, E. 'The Financing of the Lordship of Ireland under Henry V and Henry VI', in A.J. Pollard (ed.), *The Wars of the Roses*, London, 1995

Matthews, W.R. and Atkins, W.M. (eds). *A History of St Paul's Cathedral*, London, 1964

Meale, C. (ed.). *Women and Literature in Britain, 1150–1500*, Cambridge, 1993

Mertes, Kate. *The English Noble Household, 1250–1600*, Oxford, 1988

Mitchell, R.J. *John Tiptoft (1427–1470)*, London, 1938

Moreton, C.E. 'A "best betrustyd frende"?: A Late Medieval Lawyer and His Clients', *The Journal of Legal History* 11 (1990)

——. *The Townshends and Their World: Gentry, Law, and Land in Norfolk, c. 1450–1551*, Oxford, 1992

Morgan, D.A.L. 'The King's Affinity in the Polity of Yorkist England', *Transactions of the Royal Historical Society*, 5th series, XXVI (1973)

Morgan, Philip. 'The Death of Edward V and the Rebellion of 1483', *Bulletin of Historical Research*, 1995

Motley, M. *Becoming a French Aristocrat: The Education of the Court Nobility, 1580–1715*, Princeton, 1990

Mundy, J.H. and Woody, K.M. (eds). *The Council of Constance*, New York, 1961

Myers, A.R. 'The Household of Queen Margaret of Anjou, 1452–3', *Bulletin of the John Rylands Library* 40 (1957–8)

Nichols, J.G. (ed.). *The Boke of Noblesse*, London, 1860

O'Day, Rosemary. *Education and Society, 1500–1800: The Social Foundations of Education in Early Modern Britain*, London, 1982

Orme, Nicholas. *Education and Society in Medieval and Renaissance England*, London, 1989

——. *From Childhood to Chivalry: The Education of the English Kings and Aristocracy, 1066–1530*, London, 1984

Ormrod, W.M. 'The West European Monarchies in the Later Middle Ages', in R. Bonney (ed.), *Economic Systems and State Finance*, Oxford, 1995

Otway-Ruthven, A.J. *The King's Secretary and the Signet Office of the XV Century*, Cambridge, 1939

Pollard, A.J. 'St Cuthbert and the Hog: Richard III and the County Palatine of Durham, 1471', in R.A. Griffiths and J. Sherborne (eds), *Kings and Nobles in the Later Middle Ages: A Tribute to Charles Ross*, Gloucester, 1986

——. *North-Eastern England during the Wars of the Roses*, Oxford, 1990

Pollard, A.J. (ed.). *Property and Politics: Essays in Later Medieval English History*, Gloucester, 1984

——. *The Wars of the Roses*, London, 1995

Pollock, Linda. '"Teach Her to Live under Obedience": the Making of Women in the Upper Ranks of Early Modern England', *Continuity and Change* 4 (1989)

——. 'Younger Sons in Tudor and Stuart England', *History Today* 39 (June 1989)

Powell, E. 'Jury Trial at Gaol Delivery in the Late Middle Ages: The Midland Circuit, 1400–1429', in J.S. Cockburn and T.A. Green (eds), *Twelve Good Men and True: the Criminal Trial Jury in England, 1200–1800*, Princeton, N.J., 1988

——. 'The Administration of Criminal Justice in Late Medieval England: Peace Sessions and Assizes', in R. Eales and D. Sullivan (eds), *The Political Context of Law*, London, 1987

——. 'The Strange Death of Sir John Mortimer: Politics and the Law of Treason in Lancastrian England', in R.E. Archer and S. Walker (eds), *Rulers and Ruled in Late Medieval England*, London, 1995

——. *Medieval People*, London, 1963

Pronay, Nicholas and Cox, John (eds). *The Crowland Chronical Continuations: 1459–1486*, London, 1986

Pugh, T.B. 'Henry VII and the English Nobility', in G. Bernard (ed.), *The Tudor Nobility*, Manchester, 1992

——. *Henry V and the Southampton Plot of 1415*, Southampton, 1988

Raines, F.R. *A History of the Chantries within the County of Lancaster*, 2 vols, Chetham Society, 1862

Reeves, A.C. *Lancastrian Englishmen*, Washington, D.C., 1981

Richmond, C.F. '1485 and all that, or what was going on at the Battle of Bosworth', in P.W. Hammond (ed.), *Richard III: Loyalty, Lordship and Law*, London, 1986

——. 'English Naval Power in the Fifteenth Century', *History* LII (1967)

——. 'Hand and Mouth: Information Gathering and Use in England in the Later Middle Ages', *Journal of Historical Sociology* I (1988)

——. *John Hopton: A Fifteenth-Century Suffolk Gentleman*, Cambridge, 1981

——. *The Paston Family in the Fifteenth Century: Fastolf's Will*, Cambridge, 1996

——. 'The Visual Culture of Fifteenth-Century England', in A.J. Pollard, *The Wars of the Roses*, London, 1995

Rosenthal, J.T. *Late Medieval England (1377–1485): A Bibliography of Historical Scholarship, 1975–1989*, Kalamazoo, 1994

Ross, C.D. *Edward IV*, London, 1974

——. *Richard III*, London, 1981

Scofield, C.L. *The Life and Reign of Edward the Fourth*, 2 vols, London, 1923

Siddons, Michael Powell. 'Welsh Pedigree Rolls', *The National Library of Wales Journal* 29 (1996)

Simpson, A.W.B. 'The Source and Function of the Later Year Books', *Law Quarterly Review* 87 (1971)

Somerville, R. *History of the Duchy of Lancaster, 1265–1603*, London, 1953

Steel, A.B. *The Receipt of the Exchequer, 1377–1485*, Cambridge, 1954

Stevenson, J. (ed.). *Letters and Papers Illustrative of the Wars of the English in France During the Reign of Henry the Sixth*, Rolls Series, 1861–4

Stone, L. *The Crisis of the Aristocracy, 1558–1641*, Oxford, 1965

Storey, R.L. 'Wardens of the Marches of England towards Scotland, 1377–1489, *English Historical Review* 72 (1957)

——. *The Earl of the House of Lancaster*, London, 1966

——. *Thomas Langley and the Bishopric of Durham, 1406–1437*, London, 1961

Storey, R.L. (ed.). *The Register of Thomas Langley, Bishop of Durham*, 6 vols, Durham, 1949–67

Swanson, R.N. *Catholic England: Faith, Religion and Observance before the Reformation*, Manchester, 1993

Taylor, M.M. 'Justices of Assize', in J.F. Willard et al., *The English Government at Work, 1327–36*, 3 vols, Cambridge, Mass., 1950

Testamenta Eboracensia, A Selection of Wills from the Registry at York, Durham, 1869

Thomas, A.H. and Thornley, I.D. (eds). *The Great Chronicle of London*, London, 1938

Thomson, J.A.F. 'John de la Pole, duke of Suffolk', *Speculum* 54 (1979)

Thornton, T. 'Local Equity Jurisdictions in the Territories of the English Crown: the Palatinate of Chester, 1450–1550', in D. Dunn (ed.), *Courts, Counties and Capital in the Later Middle Ages*, Stroud, 1996

Tout, T.F. *Chapters in the Administrative History of Medieval England: the Wardrobe, the Chamber, and the Small Seals*, 6 vols, Manchester, 1920–3

Vale, M.G.A. *English Gascony, 1399–1453*, Oxford, 1970

Virgoe, R. 'The Earlier Knyvetts: the Rise of a Norfolk Gentry Family, Part 2', *Norfolk Archaeology* 41 (1992)

——. 'The Composition of the King's Council', *Bulletin of the Institute of Historical Research* 43 (1970)

Ward, Jennifer C. *English Nobelwomen in the Later Middle Ages*, London, 1992

Warner, G. (ed.). *The Libelle of Englyshe Polycye*, Oxford, 1926

Warnicke, R.M. *Women of the English Renaissance and Reformation*, Westport, Conn., 1983

Wedgwood, J.C. *History of Parliament: Biographies of the Members of the Commons House, 1439–1509*, London, 1936

Wernham, R.B. *Before the Armada: The Growth of English Foreign Policy, 1485–1588*, London, 1966

Willard, J.F. et al. *The English Government at Work, 1327–1336*, 3 vols, Cambridge, Mass., 1950

Wills and Inventories Illustrative of the History, Manners, Language, Statistics etc. of the Northern Counties of England, from the Eleventh Century Downwards, London, 1835

Windeatt, B.A., trans. *The Book of Margery Kempe*, London, 1985

Wolffe, B.P. *Henry VI*, London, 1981

——. *The Crown Lands, 1461 to 1536*, London, 1970

——. *The Royal Demesne in English History to 1509*, London, 1971

Woodbridge, Linda. *Women and the Renaissance: Literature and the Nature of Womankind, 1540–1620*, Urbana, Ill., 1986

Wright, Thomas. *Feudal Manuals of English History*, London, 1872

INDEX